THE QUICK ROASTING TIN

30 MINUTE ONE DISH DINNERS

FOR MAMIE, 1924-2017

THE QUICK
ROASTING TIN

30 MINUTE ONE DISH DINNERS

RUKMINI IYER

10 9 8 7

Square Peg, an imprint of Vintage,
20 Vauxhall Bridge Road,
London SW1V 2SA

Square Peg is part of the Penguin Random House group
of companies whose addresses can be found at:
global.penguinrandomhouse.com

First published by Square Peg in 2019
Penguin.co.uk/vintage

A CIP catalogue record for this book is available
from the British Library

ISBN 9781529110067

Patterned paper background designs for photographs
were granted with kind permission as follows:
Pages 27, 87, 119, 131, 159, 199, 213, 215: BungalowDK ©
Pages 9, 53, 61, 105, 135, 139, 173, 187, 217: Cambridge Imprint ©
Pages 13, 14, 35, 93, 147, 179: Esme Winter ©

Design & prop styling by Pene Parker
Photography by David Loftus
Food styling by Rukmini Iyer
Food styling assistant Alex Dorgan
Printed and bound in Italy by L.E.G.O. S.p.A.

Penguin Random House is committed to a sustainable future
for our business, our readers and our planet.
This book is made from Forest Stewardship Council® certified paper.

CONTENTS

INTRODUCTION

As a food stylist, I'm surrounded by food on photo shoots all day, ranging from the simplest of salads and pastas to the most complicated dishes, like one chef's interpretation of a roast dinner involving six-hour confit of the bird's legs, a stock from the bones, and a brine for the crown involving six different types of peppercorn. And that's before the four deconstructed side dishes. But from my experience around all of these different types of food and working in the food industry, I have found that come lunchtime, when we stop to try the dishes from the morning, it's the simplest things that people enjoy the most. It's those dishes that people want the recipe for, and that I'll make at home on the weekend. I am therefore a signed-up advocate for simple food.

In accordance with this, more often than not, I turn to one tin cooking at home. One tin dishes which need a minimal stint in the oven are even better, because I am greedy and want dinner to prepare itself quickly and without my attendance. We all have busy lives and things to do when we get home before we've thought about what to cook but I strongly believe that having time constraints in the kitchen doesn't mean that you have to compromise on flavour, texture or interest in your food. That's why this collection of roasting tin recipes maintains the trademark vibrancy of my first two cookbooks, but I've developed recipes here which can all be cooked in the oven within 30 minutes (and many in even less time). There's 10 minutes or so of light prep and then you'll have up to 30 minutes, while dinner looks after itself, to supervise homework, watch something on Netflix or take a nice hot bath.

You can find all the ingredients for the recipes in a big supermarket, because that makes up the majority of what's in my cupboard. Luckily, that doesn't exclude too many interesting options, thanks to stellar cookbook authors who've made varied types of cooking accessible. About three quarters of the recipes in this book are vegetarian or vegan, which I think reflects the way that many people cook nowadays. While there's plenty for omnivores, many of the recipes involve bacon, pancetta, chorizo or ham hock as a flavouring rather than as the main

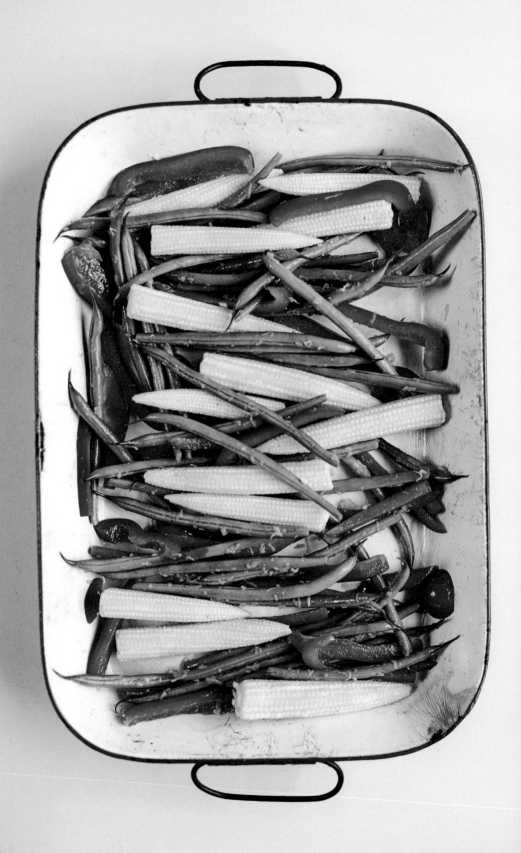

ingredient, so they can be easily left out, and replaced with my go-to goat's cheese, halloumi or feta.

The chapters in this book are organised by occasion. The first is full of simple dishes that you can put together on a weeknight after work, with largely storecupboard ingredients plus one or two bits grabbed from the supermarket on the way home. The crispy thyme roasted leek & mushroom pasta bake (page 24) and Kerala prawn curry (page 32) are already favourites among my friends.

The next chapter of the book is on family favourites, because one of the nicest things to come out of the first two Roasting Tin books is the number of new parents who have written to me to say how helpful the recipes are when juggling babies and zooming toddlers and even for baby-lead weaning. The tins in this chapter are designed to ideally feed both you and your children, on the basis of a very scientific straw poll among parent friends and colleagues as to what their children will and won't eat. As you'll see from the chapter, there was an overwhelming 'yes' to peas, a surprising positive on broccoli, and a loud 'no' to mushrooms. I apologise if your children disagree, but feel free to mix and match ingredients according to their tastes and if they still object, all the more in the tin for you to eat. The quick meatball pizza (page 58) is a good one to cook if you have helpers with small hands, and the baked gnocchi with crispy ham hock & peas (page 50) is an instant staple.

As I love recipes that make enough for dinner as well as a couple of lunches during the week, the third chapter is dedicated to make ahead lunchboxes, packed with easy, grain based dishes that you can batch cook at the weekend, like the tikka-spiced paneer salad with chickpeas, mint & naan croutons (page 90), or the super quick orzo gardiniera with courgettes, chilli and lemon (page 96).

The date night chapter is full of visually beautiful, delicious one tin recipes which have slightly more special ingredients, but take no more effort to make than any other one tin dish.

Chapter five focuses on easy entertaining: roasting tin dishes that you can scale up to feed a crowd. I've been making more Indian food recently, so this chapter includes tandoori-style salmon with spiced, roasted sweet potatoes, tomatoes & red onion (page 146) and masala roasted corn with quick coriander chutney (page 156), which I could happily eat every day.

Lazy weekend cooking makes up chapter six. Your tins will still take 30 minutes in the oven, but if you have time for a little contemplative food production, you'll find the delicious pork, juniper & pink peppercorn meatballs with leeks and Puy lentils (page 188), along with my proudest creation, a crisp cheddar-topped bread cobbler with chilli spiked greens (page 176). Finally, there's a chapter on desserts, because I do like a pudding, and there's enough here to sort you for a weekend baking session or to finish off a dinner party.

This is my favourite collection of roasting tin recipes to date, not only because the dishes have already become staples, but also because I think that good food should be achievable however little time you have. As with my other Roasting Tin books, this cookbook is for people who like good food, without any hassle. Pick your recipe, do a bit of light chopping and an interesting, flavourful dinner will be ready in 30 minutes or less. It's minimum effort, maximum return cooking.

A NOTE ON TINS

The key message is that you can use any kind. Pyrex lasagne dishes, ceramic dishes, the bottom half of a large Le Creuset, enamel tins, stainless steel tins, even the big tray that comes fitted in your oven.

What you'll want to bear in mind, particularly for efficient 30-minute cooking, is that you need to use a tin large enough for all your vegetables to fit in a single layer. If they pile up on top of each other, the ingredients underneath will steam, not roast, and may not cook in 30 minutes. Grains that go underneath the veg in stock aren't as fussy, and meat can sit on top of veg, if needed.

Most of the recipes in the book will suggest a size for the roasting tin in terms of fitting all the ingredients in one layer. I made pretty much everything in my 30ish x 37cm roasting tins. If in doubt, go large.

A NOTE ON OVENS

Every oven is different. I was fascinated to learn that top oven manufacturers employ home economists to bake a tray of equally measured, standard British fairy cakes in their prototype ovens, to check for hot and cold spots depending on which cakes brown more, and then adjust the ovens accordingly to provide an even heat. (Sadly, I've never met one of these evenly browning ovens in real life, please advise if you have.) Cheffy types often use oven thermometers, which sit in your oven to tell you the exact temperature on the inside, which is almost always different from the temperature to which you turn the dial on the outside. (The oven in my mother's kitchen runs 10–20°C hotter than mine, so we often reduce either the temperature or the cooking time. The one at my sister's flat runs 10–20°C colder, so she usually adds 5–10 minutes to the cooking time.)

If you have an oven thermometer, by all means use it. But I don't think it's necessary to get too science-ey with roasting tin dinners. If you're already familiar with your oven, you may instinctively know to turn the dial up or down a bit more to allow for its foibles. If you're not a habitual oven user, it's easy enough to pick a simple recipe (cakes are good as it is very easy to objectively see how cooked they are within an allotted time), make a note of the results, then the next time adjust the temperature or cooking time up or down as needed.

All the recipes in my three Roasting Tin books have been tested for oven timings in my oven at home, many in my mother's kitchen, a good proportion at friend's houses, an endearing number by the team at VINTAGE books and all of them in the oven where we shot the photographs you see in the book. If you find that the recipes consistently cook in more or less time in your oven, consider that it may be the oven and adjust the temperature or the timings as needed.

WORKNIGHT DINNERS

STORECUPBOARD INGREDIENTS
& A COUPLE OF THINGS FROM THE
SUPERMARKET ON THE WAY HOME

WORKNIGHT DINNERS

STICKY SOY & HONEY ROASTED SALMON
WITH ASPARAGUS & SUGAR SNAP PEAS

CRISPY THYME ROASTED LEEK
& MUSHROOM PASTA BAKE (V)

ALL-IN-ONE THAI FISH PIE

ROSEMARY, GOAT'S CHEESE & MUSHROOM TART
WITH PINK PEPPERCORNS (V)

KERALA PRAWN CURRY

BEETROOT ORZOTTO WITH SOURED CREAM,
PINE NUTS & DILL (V)

CHILLI PEANUT BEEF WITH RED PEPPERS,
SWEETCORN & SPRING ONIONS

SESAME CRUSTED TUNA WITH SOY
& GINGER, COURGETTES & PAK CHOI

CHERRY TOMATO, LEEK & ARTICHOKE BAKE
WITH FETA CHEESE (V)

QUICK COOK CAULIFLOWER CURRY
WITH PEAS & SPINACH (VEGAN)

CRISPY BAKED GNOCCHI WITH LEEKS,
RAINBOW CHARD & CREAM (V)

STICKY SOY & HONEY ROASTED SALMON
WITH ASPARAGUS & SUGAR SNAP PEAS

This easy, flavourful dish is perfect for a quick worknight dinner. If you're serving fewer people, I'd think about making the full quantity and taking any leftovers for lunch the next day. Serve as it is for a carb-free dinner, or with rice or quick cook noodles.

Serves: 4
Prep: 5 minutes
Cook: 25 minutes

200g Tenderstem broccoli
125g asparagus spears
200g sugar snap peas
200g frozen peas
1 teaspoon sea salt flakes
1 tablespoon sesame oil
Quick cook noodles or rice,
  to serve (optional)

FOR THE SALMON
4 salmon fillets
1/2 tablespoon good soy sauce
1/2 tablespoon sesame oil
1/2 tablespoon honey

FOR THE DRESSING
6cm fresh ginger, grated
1 lime, juice only
1 tablespoon sesame oil
3 spring onions, finely chopped
A handful of peanuts, roughly
  chopped
1 red chilli, finely sliced

Preheat the oven to 180°C fan/200°C/gas 6. Put the broccoli into a large bowl, pour over a kettleful of boiling water, leave to stand for 1 minute, then drain well.

Mix the broccoli, asparagus, sugar snaps, frozen peas, sea salt and sesame oil in a roasting tin. Put the salmon fillets in around the veg, then mix the soy, sesame oil and honey and spread this over each fillet. Roast for 20–25 minutes until the salmon is cooked through.

Meanwhile, whisk the ginger, lime juice, sesame oil and spring onions together. Once the salmon is cooked, pour the dressing over the vegetables. Scatter over the chopped peanuts and chilli. Taste and adjust the lime juice and salt as needed and serve hot.

NOTE: I've said to blanch the Tenderstem as it improves the texture on roasting, but you can use ordinary broccoli instead if you prefer and skip this stage.

CRISPY THYME ROASTED LEEK & MUSHROOM PASTA BAKE

This is soothing comfort food, based on a dish my mother used to make at home. I like using tagliatelle, as it's unusual in a pasta bake, but by all means substitute your favourite pasta shape. My friend Emma reports that fusilli works well. Speed up your cooking by prepping the vegetables as the pasta cooks, then it's just a quick stint in the oven to finish.

Serves: 2–3
Prep: 10 minutes
Cook: 30 minutes

200g tagliatelle
2 large leeks,
   cut into $\frac{1}{2}$ cm half moons
250g chestnut mushrooms,
   roughly sliced
300ml crème fraîche
1 tablespoon olive oil,
   plus more to bake
1 teaspoon sea salt flakes
10 sprigs of fresh thyme,
   leaves only
75g cheddar cheese, grated
100g panko breadcrumbs

Preheat the oven to 200°C fan/220°C/gas 7. Cook the pasta in a large pan of boiling salted water for 10 minutes, until just cooked but still al dente. (If you're using fresh tagliatelle from the chiller section of the supermarket, it's usually just 3–4 minutes.)

While the pasta is cooking, slice the leeks and mushrooms and grate the cheddar. Drop the leeks in with the pasta water for the last minute of cooking, then drain well.

Tip the pasta and leeks into a roasting tin or lasagne dish and stir through the crème fraîche, olive oil, sea salt and half the thyme leaves. Top with the sliced mushrooms and the remaining thyme, followed by the grated cheddar and the breadcrumbs.

Drizzle over a little more olive oil, then transfer to the oven and bake for 15–20 minutes, until the top is golden brown and crisp. Serve hot, with a green salad if you like.

ALL-IN-ONE THAI FISH PIE

This is such a quick but flavoursome one pot dinner. The fish gently poaches with the coconut cream, lemongrass and lime leaves, while the crunchy filo topping provides a lovely textural contrast. It's worth getting fresh Kaffir lime leaves if you can – a couple of large supermarkets stock them with the fresh herbs – but use dried from the spice aisle if not.

Serves: 2 generously
Prep: 10 minutes
Cook: 25 minutes

300g fish pie mix
   (or a mix of salmon, smoked
   haddock and cod, cut into
   4cm chunks)
1 small head of broccoli,
   cut into small florets
1 stick lemongrass
2 Kaffir lime leaves
1 x 160g tin of coconut cream
1 lime, zest and juice
$\frac{1}{2}$ tablespoon fish sauce
Pinch of sea salt flakes
3 sheets of filo pastry
$1\frac{1}{2}$ tablespoons olive oil,
   or olive oil spray

Preheat the oven to 180C°fan/200°C/gas 6. Tip the fish and broccoli into a small deep roasting tin with the lemongrass and lime leaves, then pour over the coconut cream, lime zest and juice and fish sauce.

Scatter over a pinch of salt, then scrumple the filo pastry sheets over the fish. Brush the pastry with olive oil (or spritz with olive oil spray), then transfer to the oven and bake for 25 minutes, until the pastry is golden brown and crisp. Serve hot.

NOTE: If your fish pie mix is frozen, you'll want to defrost it under plenty of cold running water, then pat the fish dry before putting it into the pie, otherwise too much liquid gets released. (That's why I suggest coconut cream instead of coconut milk, as it's much thicker.)

ROSEMARY, GOAT'S CHEESE & MUSHROOM TART WITH PINK PEPPERCORNS

This tart is inspired by Remy from the film *Ratatouille*, who spears rosemary, a perfect mushroom and a piece of cheese together before lovingly toasting them over a smoking chimney. I'm sure he would have approved of the addition of pink peppercorns, they're easy to find next to ordinary pepper at the supermarket and add a wonderful aromatic flavour as well as a vibrant pop of colour.

Serves: 2 generously
Prep: 10 minutes
Cook: 25 minutes

200g brown chestnut
  mushrooms, roughly sliced
1 tablespoon olive oil
3 sprigs of fresh rosemary,
  leaves finely chopped
2 heaped tablespoons
  crème fraîche
1 x 320g ready-rolled
  puff pastry sheet
2 x 125g goat's cheese logs, sliced
2 teaspoons or so pink
  peppercorns
A handful of fresh flat-leaf
  parsley, finely chopped

FOR THE SALAD
100g baby leaf spinach
1 tablespoon extra virgin olive oil
$1/2$ a lemon, juice only
A pinch of sea salt

Preheat the oven to 180°C fan/200°C/gas 6. Mix the mushrooms in a bowl with the olive oil and half the rosemary.

Spread the crème fraîche over the puff pastry, leaving a 1cm border. Top with the remaining chopped rosemary, the mushrooms, then the sliced goat's cheese. Transfer to the oven and bake for 25 minutes, until the edges are a deep golden brown and crisp.

Just before the tart is ready, toss the spinach with the extra virgin olive oil, the lemon juice and sea salt and set aside.

Once the tart is crisp and cooked through, scatter over the pink peppercorns and chopped flat-leaf parsley, and serve with the spinach salad alongside.

CHANGE IT UP: If you have friends round and are looking for an easy starter, you can make this as four individual tarts by cutting the pastry into smaller rectangles.

KERALA PRAWN CURRY

This aromatic prawn curry in coconut milk with storecupboard ingredients is a perfect weeknight dinner. Serve it with flatbreads, naan or fluffy white basmati rice. I usually pull it together with a bag of frozen prawns from the freezer (defrost them in plenty of cold running water just before cooking them), so you only need to grab a few fresh ingredients on the way home.

Serves: 2–3
Prep: 10 minutes
Cook: 30 minutes

220g cherry tomatoes on the vine, halved
1 green pepper, finely sliced
1 onion, roughly sliced
2cm fresh ginger, grated
2 teaspoons mustard seeds
1 teaspoon freshly ground black pepper
1 teaspoon ground coriander
1 heaped teaspoon ground cumin
$1/2$ teaspoon ground turmeric
1 teaspoon ground chilli
A few curry leaves (optional)
1 teaspoon sea salt
1 tablespoon oil
1 x 400g tin of coconut milk
300–350g raw king prawns
100g spinach, roughly chopped
1 lime, juice only

TO SERVE
A handful of fresh coriander, roughly chopped
1 red chilli, finely chopped

Preheat the oven to 180°C fan/200°C/gas 6. Tip the tomatoes and their vines, the green pepper, onion, ginger, all the spices, salt and oil into a roasting tin and mix really well to coat everything evenly.

Transfer the tin to the oven and roast for 15–20 minutes (if your oven runs hot and things start to char, rescue them after 15).

Fish out the vines, squash down the tomatoes, add the coconut milk, prawns and spinach and return to the oven for 9–10 minutes, or until the prawns are pink and just cooked through.

Taste and season with the lime juice and more salt as needed, scatter over the fresh coriander and chopped chilli to taste and serve with flatbreads or white basmati rice.

CHANGE IT UP: If you prefer a thicker curry, use half the amount of coconut milk, or a 200g can of coconut cream. (Don't make the mistake I have in the past and buy a cardboard packet of creamed coconut, it's useful only as a cosh/doorstop.)

BEETROOT ORZOTTO WITH SOURED CREAM, PINE NUTS & DILL

This vibrantly pink orzo dish takes just minutes to put together – if you don't mind grating a bit of fresh beetroot – and tastes as good as it looks. You could substitute blue, feta or goat's cheese for the soured cream if you have some in the fridge, but having tried this topped with a variety of cheeses/nuts/levels-of-lemon-juice, soured cream and pine nuts won out against the earthy beetroot.

Serves: 2
Prep: 10 minutes
Cook: 20 minutes

200g orzo
500ml vegetable stock
1 tablespoon olive oil
300g fresh beetroot, peeled
    and grated
A handful of beetroot stems,
    finely chopped
50g pine nuts
150g soured cream
    or crème fraîche
1 tablespoon extra virgin olive oil
1 lemon, juice only
1 teaspoon sea salt flakes
A handful of fresh dill, finely
    chopped
Freshly ground black pepper

Preheat the oven to 180°C fan/200°C/gas 6. Tip the orzo, vegetable stock and oil into a medium-sized roasting tin, then top evenly with the grated beetroot and chopped stems. Scatter over the pine nuts, then transfer to the oven and cook for 20 minutes.

After 20 minutes, the orzo should be cooked through but still al dente. If it's not cooked to your liking, return it to the oven for a further 5 minutes.

Stir through all but a couple of tablespoons of the soured cream or crème fraîche, the extra virgin olive oil and lemon juice, then taste and add the salt as needed (I add quite a bit because I feel the beetroot can take it, but you may prefer less).

Serve with the remaining soured cream or crème fraîche, a scattering of dill and freshly ground black pepper.

CHILLI PEANUT BEEF WITH RED PEPPERS, SWEETCORN & SPRING ONIONS

Think about your favourite stir-fry. Now think about making it without having to stand and stir. This dish has gone straight to the top of my list – not only does the beef, pepper and sweetcorn combination cook beautifully in the oven, but the peanut-soy dressing is addictive – and I'd happily eat it in sandwiches.

Serves: 2
Prep: 10 minutes
Cook: 25 minutes

400g free-range rump steak,
  sliced into 1 $\frac{1}{2}$ cm slices
200g green beans
175g baby sweetcorn
1 red pepper, finely sliced
1 red chilli, finely grated
2 cloves of garlic, finely grated
5cm fresh ginger, grated
1 teaspoon sea salt flakes
1 tablespoon sesame oil

FOR THE DRESSING
45g crunchy peanut butter
1 tablespoon dark soy sauce
1 tablespoon rice vinegar or
  lime juice
1 tablespoon water

TO SERVE
50g spinach, roughly chopped
3 spring onions, finely sliced
A handful of salted peanuts,
  roughly chopped
Quick cook noodles or rice

Preheat the oven to 200°C fan/220°C/gas 7. Tip the sliced steak, green beans, sweetcorn and pepper into a roasting tin large enough to hold all the veg in a single layer. Add the grated chilli, garlic, ginger, sea salt and sesame oil and mix to make sure everything is coated.

Move the slices of steak to the top of the tin, as you want them to char nicely, then transfer to the oven to roast for 25 minutes.

Meanwhile, mix the peanut butter, soy sauce and rice vinegar or lime juice with the water. Once the beef is cooked, stir through the spinach, pour over the dressing, scatter with the spring onions and salted peanuts and serve with the cooked noodles or rice.

NOTE: If you want to get the sliced spring onions really crisp and take away a bit of the 'onion-y' flavour, stick them in a bowl of cold water for 10 minutes, then drain well.

SESAME CRUSTED TUNA WITH SOY & GINGER, COURGETTES & PAK CHOI

This might look like a light meal, but with the addition of cannellini beans (taking the place of a carb, as they work so beautifully with tuna and require no effort), it's incredibly filling as well as delicious. With the quick cooking time, the courgettes retain their crunch and freshness. I imagine this will quickly become a weeknight favourite in your house, as it is in mine.

Serves: 2
Prep: 10 minutes
Cook: 15 minutes

200g courgettes, halved
   and cut into $\frac{1}{2}$ cm half moons
2 heads of pak choi, quartered,
   or cut into 8 if large
$3\frac{1}{2}$ tablespoons sesame oil
2 nice tuna steaks
   (about 240g in total)
1 heaped teaspoon each black
   and white sesame seeds
   (or just use whichever you
   have in the cupboard)
2 tablespoons rice vinegar
   or lime juice
2 tablespoons soy sauce
4cm fresh ginger, grated
1 scant teaspoon chilli flakes
1 x 400g tin of cannellini beans,
   drained and rinsed

Preheat the oven to 200°C fan/220°C/gas 7. Mix the courgettes and pak choi in a roasting tin along with 1 tablespoon of the sesame oil. Lay the tuna steaks on top and gently rub them with another $\frac{1}{2}$ tablespoon of sesame oil. Scatter the steaks with the sesame seeds, then transfer to the oven and roast for 10-15 minutes until the tuna is just cooked through.

Meanwhile, mix the remaining 2 tablespoons of sesame oil, the rice vinegar or lime juice, soy sauce, ginger and chilli flakes together in a big bowl. Reserve a couple of tablespoons of dressing, then stir the cannellini beans through the rest of the dressing in the bowl.

Once the tuna is cooked to your liking, stir the cannellini beans through the vegetables, dress the fish with those reserved tablespoons of dressing and serve hot.

CHANGE IT UP: This dish is also lovely with baby courgettes.

CHERRY TOMATO, LEEK & ARTICHOKE BAKE WITH FETA CHEESE

Think of this as a cross between a frittata, a toad-in-the-hole and a delicious giant savoury pancake. It contains too much feta cheese to puff up like a Yorkshire pudding, but then there's arguably no such thing as too much cheese and it gives a wonderful flavour to the dish.

Serves: 2–3
Prep: 10 minutes
Cook: 30 minutes

2 leeks, finely sliced
2 tablespoons olive oil
200g plain flour
3 free-range eggs
300ml milk
200g feta cheese, crumbled
250g cherry tomatoes on the vine
1 x 290g jar sliced artichoke
   hearts, drained
15g fresh dill, roughly chopped
Lemon-dressed spinach salad,
   to serve (see page 30)

Preheat the oven to 210°C fan/230°C/gas 8. While it's heating, slice the leeks, tip them into a metal roasting tin along with the oil, mix well, then pop them into the oven to roast while you get on with the batter.

Meanwhile, put the flour into a bowl. Whisk the eggs and milk together, pour this over the flour and whisk until smooth, then stir in the crumbled feta cheese.

Once the oven has come to temperature, remove the tin of leeks, give them a good stir, then pour the batter evenly over the top. Scatter over the tomatoes, their vines and the artichokes, then return to the oven and cook for 25–30 minutes, until the bake is well risen and golden brown.

Serve hot, scattered with the dill, with the lemon-dressed spinach salad alongside.

QUICK COOK CAULIFLOWER CURRY
WITH PEAS & SPINACH

One of my favourite dishes at home is my mother's cauliflower, potato and pea curry, known as 'chechki' and seasoned with Bengali five-spice. Alas, every variation I made with potatoes resolutely refused to cook within 30 minutes, so I've adapted it to this colourful, child-friendly version with quick cook cherry tomatoes and coconut milk.

Serves: 2–3
Prep: 10 minutes
Cook: 30 minutes

2 teaspoons mustard seeds
2 teaspoons fennel seeds
2 teaspoon cumin seeds
2 teaspoon nigella
  (black onion) seeds
1 cauliflower, cut into small florets
Leaves from the cauliflower,
  finely chopped
220g cherry tomatoes, halved
1 red onion, sliced into 8
2 cloves of garlic, crushed
5cm fresh ginger, grated
1 tablespoon oil
1 teaspoon sea salt flakes
200g frozen peas
80g spinach, roughly chopped
1 x 400g tin of coconut milk

TO SERVE
1 lime, juice only
A handful of fresh coriander,
  roughly chopped
Rice or flatbreads

Preheat the oven to 200°C fan/220°C/gas 7. Bash the mustard, fennel, cumin and nigella seeds in a pestle and mortar and then tip them into a roasting tin with everything except the spinach and coconut milk. (Use a a roasting tin large enough to hold all the vegetables in a single layer.) Transfer the tin to the oven to roast for 20 minutes.

Stir through the chopped spinach and coconut milk and let everything cook for a further 10 minutes until the cauliflower is cooked through.

Season with the lime juice, then taste and adjust the salt as needed (I think this dish can take a lot of salt, but then I am a salt fiend). Scatter everything with fresh coriander before serving hot, with rice or flatbreads.

NOTE: Be sure to cut the cauliflower into small florets so that it cooks through in 30 minutes.

CRISPY BAKED GNOCCHI WITH LEEKS, RAINBOW CHARD & CREAM

Baked gnocchi is my new favourite dish, and I've been putting everything in it: spring greens, mushrooms, broccoli. . . It's also perfect for using up odds and ends of cheese left over in the fridge. (For some reason, the combination of Dijon mustard and Swiss chard in this recipe reminded me of bacon, even though it's completely vegetarian, so it's a good dish for meat-free Mondays, or for veggies with nostalgia.)

Serves: 3-4
Prep: 10 minutes
Cook: 20 minutes

2 leeks, sliced into
    $1/2$ cm half moons
200g rainbow or Swiss chard,
    roughly sliced
500g gnocchi
250ml double cream
2 heaped teaspoons Dijon
    mustard
1 teaspoon sea salt flakes
Freshly ground black pepper
125g soft goat's cheese log,
    crumbled
50g panko breadcrumbs
1 tablespoon olive oil

Preheat the oven to 200°C fan/220°C/gas 7. Tip the leeks, sliced chard and gnocchi into a large bowl, pour a kettleful of boiling water over them and leave to stand for 2 minutes. Drain really well, then tip the veg and gnocchi into a roasting tin large enough to sit everything in a single layer.

Stir through the double cream and Dijon mustard and season with the sea salt and freshly ground black pepper. Scatter over the goat's cheese, then the panko breadcrumbs and drizzle with the olive oil.

Transfer to the oven and bake for 15–20 minutes, until the top is golden brown and crisp. Serve hot.

FAMILY FAVOURITES

SOOTHING, CHILD-FRIENDLY
WEEKNIGHT DINNERS

FAMILY FAVOURITES

BAKED GNOCCHI WITH CRISPY HAM HOCK & PEAS

QUICK CHICKEN, LEEK & CHORIZO PIE

CRISPY BAKED COD WITH HERBY BROCCOLI,
PEAS & BEANS

SUMMER SAUSAGE TRAYBAKE WITH LONG-STEM
BROCCOLI & CHERRY TOMATOES

QUICK MEATBALL PIZZA WITH CHERRY TOMATOES
& MOZZARELLA

SPICED SWEET POTATO CURRY
WITH PEAS & COCONUT MILK (VEGAN)

ROASTED BROCCOLI & BACON CONCHIGLIE BAKE
WITH CRÈME FRAÎCHE

SIMPLE ROASTED PEPPER ORZOTTO (VEGAN)

QUICK COOK CAULIFLOWER CHEESE
WITH CRÈME FRAÎCHE, MUSTARD & KALE (V)

ALL-IN-ONE NIGELLA-SPICED
WHOLE TOMATO DHAL (VEGAN)

ROASTED AUBERGINE, COURGETTE
& MACARONI BAKE (V)

BAKED GNOCCHI WITH CRISPY HAM HOCK & PEAS

What's better than baked gnocchi? Baked gnocchi with crispy ham hock on top. This simple family-friendly dinner is perfect for a quick, easy weeknight meal: all the major food groups in one tin.

Serves: 4 generously
Prep: 10 minutes
Cook: 25 minutes

500g gnocchi
400g frozen peas
300g crème fraîche
1 tablespoon Dijon mustard
$\frac{1}{2}$ teaspoon sea salt flakes
(optional)
Freshly ground black pepper
180g shredded free-range
ham hock
$\frac{1}{2}$ lemon, juice only
A handful of flat-leaf parsley
leaves, finely chopped

Preheat the oven to 180°C fan/200°C/gas 6. Put the gnocchi into a large bowl and pour over a kettleful of boiling water. Let it stand for 2 minutes, then drain well and tip the gnocchi into a roasting tin along with the peas, crème fraîche, mustard, salt (if using) and freshly ground black pepper.

Mix everything well in the tin, then scatter the shredded ham hock evenly all over. Grind over a little more black pepper, then transfer to the oven and bake for 25 minutes, until the ham is nicely crisped.

Squeeze over the lemon juice, scatter over the flat-leaf parsley and serve hot.

QUICK CHICKEN, LEEK & CHORIZO PIE

This chicken pie went through several elaborate variations (saffron and pearl barley, anyone?) before I came up with this very simple version and rather nervously handed platefuls to my friends Ruby and Leah. Fortunately, it turned out beautifully and was by far the easiest to make. A new weeknight staple.

Serves: 4
Prep: 10 minutes
Cook: 25–30 minutes

2 leeks, very finely sliced
4 small free-range chicken
   breasts, cut into large chunks
120g chorizo, diced
300g crème fraîche
1/2 a juicy lemon, zest and juice
1 teaspoon sea salt flakes
   (optional)
Freshly ground black pepper
1 free-range egg, beaten
1 x 320g ready-rolled
   puff pastry sheet

Preheat the oven to 180°C fan/200°C/gas 6. Tip the leeks into a bowl, pour over a kettleful of boiling water, and leave to steep for 2 minutes while you get on with prepping the other ingredients.

Drain the leeks well in a colander, then tip into a roasting tin along with the chopped chicken, chorizo, crème fraiche, lemon zest and juice, salt (if using) and a good grind of black pepper. Give everything a good mix, then brush the edges of the roasting tin with a little beaten egg and lay the pastry on top.

Use your thumbs or a fork to press the edges of the pastry against the edges of the tin – don't worry about any overhang, it'll just mean there's more to eat later. Brush with the beaten egg, then cut a cross in the middle for steam to escape. You can add cut shapes from the excess pastry and stick them on top with a little beaten egg, if you're feeling artistic.

Transfer to the oven and bake for 25–30 minutes, until the pastry is crisp and golden brown. Let the pie sit for 5 minutes before serving hot.

CHANGE IT UP: This pie is also excellent without chorizo, as leeks pack in so much flavour. Consider adding a couple of teaspoons of Dijon mustard instead.

CRISPY BAKED COD WITH HERBY BROCCOLI, PEAS & BEANS

This is such an easy week-night dish, with mostly storecupboard ingredients: pesto, breadcrumbs, frozen peas. Adding a tin of butter beans (by all means use cannellini, haricot or Puy lentils if that's what you have) picks up all the flavour from the roasting tin. Serve with good crusty bread for an additional carb.

Serves: 2 adults + 2 children
Prep: 10 minutes
Cook: 20–25 minutes

300g Tenderstem broccoli
300g frozen peas
2 courgettes, cut into $\frac{1}{2}$cm
   half moons
2 tablespoons olive oil
1 teaspoon sea salt (optional)
Freshly ground black pepper
4 cod fillets
4 teaspoons green pesto
4 heaped tablespoons panko
   or white breadcrumbs
1 x 400g tin of butter beans,
   drained and rinsed
$\frac{1}{2}$ a lemon, zest and juice
A large bunch of fresh basil
   leaves, finely chopped

Preheat the oven to 180°C fan/200°C/gas 6. Pop the Tenderstem into a bowl, tip a kettleful of boiling water over it and leave to sit for 2 minutes, then drain well. (If the stems are very thick, halve them lengthways.) If using ordinary broccoli, skip this step.

Mix the broccoli, frozen peas and courgettes in a large roasting tin along with 1$\frac{1}{2}$ tablespoons of the olive oil, the sea salt (if using) and a good grind of black pepper. I like to add the butter beans at the end, to just warm through in the residual heat of the roasting tin, but if you'd prefer them piping hot, stick them in now.

Lay the cod fillets over the vegetables, spread each with 1 teaspoon of pesto, scatter over the breadcrumbs, then drizzle with the remaining $\frac{1}{2}$ tablespoon of olive oil. Grind over some black pepper, then transfer to the oven and roast for 20–25 minutes (20 if your cod fillets are quite thin, 25 if they are a little thicker).

Once cooked, stir in the butter beans (if you haven't already), lemon zest, juice and fresh basil and serve hot.

SUMMER SAUSAGE TRAYBAKE WITH LONG-STEM BROCCOLI & CHERRY TOMATOES

I usually think of sausage bakes as wintery dishes, but they work just as well with fresh courgettes, tomatoes and broccoli for a light, summery dinner.

Serves: 2 adults + 2 children
Prep: 10 minutes
Cook: 30 minutes

250g Tenderstem broccoli
500g courgettes,
  cut into 1/2cm slices
300g cherry tomatoes on
  the vine
1 red onion, finely sliced
1 1/2 tablespoons olive oil
2 cloves of garlic, crushed
2–3 sprigs of fresh rosemary
1 teaspoon sea salt flakes
  (optional)
1 teaspoon chilli flakes
  (optional: leave out for children)
8–12 free-range chipolata
  sausages

TO SERVE
1 lemon, juice only

Preheat the oven to 210°C fan/230°C/gas 8. Put the broccoli into a large bowl, pour over a kettleful of boiling water, leave to stand for 1 minute, then drain well. If using ordinary broccoli, skip this step.

Tip everything into a roasting tin large enough to hold it all in a single layer, and mix well. Make sure the sausages are on top, then transfer to the oven and bake for 30 minutes.

If your oven heats unevenly, turn the roasting tin after about 20 minutes so the sausages brown evenly.

Squeeze a little lemon juice and sea salt over the vegetables to taste and serve hot.

QUICK MEATBALL PIZZA WITH CHERRY TOMATOES & MOZZARELLA

This stunning, unashamedly loaded pizza-style tart is possibly one of my proudest creations. And it's an opportunity to use nigella or black onion seeds, which are my new favourite spice, not just because they share a name with my favourite cookery writer, but because they work particularly well with tomatoes and puff pastry.

Serves: 4
Prep: 10 minutes
Cook: 25–30 minutes

400g free-range minced beef, lamb or pork
1 teaspoon sea salt (optional)
1 shallot, roughly chopped
2 teaspoons nigella (black onion) seeds
1 x 320g ready-rolled puff pastry sheet
3 tablespoons chopped tinned tomatoes
1 clove of garlic, crushed
100g cherry tomatoes, halved
100g broccoli, cut into small florets (can be Tenderstem)
1 x 150g ball of mozzarella cheese, torn
Fresh basil leaves, to serve

NOTE: Don't panic if it looks like you can't possibly fit all the veg and mozzarella on top of the tart as you assemble, everything shrinks on cooking.

Preheat the oven to 180°C fan/200°C/gas 6. Tip the minced meat, $\frac{1}{2}$ teaspoon of salt (if using), shallot and half the nigella seeds into a food processor, and blitz until mixed. (Alternatively, finely chop the shallot and mix in a bowl.)

Roll the minced meat into 18 or so small walnut-sized meatballs, or get little hands to help you with this. It's easier with damp hands, so keep a bowl of water nearby.

Unroll the puff pastry into a roasting tin or on to a large baking sheet, leaving it on the paper that it comes wrapped in. Mix the tinned tomatoes with the crushed garlic, remaining nigella seeds and another $\frac{1}{2}$ teaspoon of salt (if using), and spread this all over the pastry, leaving a $1\frac{1}{2}$ cm border around the edges.

Dot the meatballs all over the pizza, then arrange the cherry tomatoes and broccoli in between. Scatter everything with the mozzarella, then transfer to the oven and bake for 25–30 minutes, until the edges are golden brown and crisp and the meatballs cooked through. Scatter over the basil and serve hot.

SPICED SWEET POTATO CURRY
WITH PEAS & COCONUT MILK

This curry is a real crowd-pleaser, with just a little bit of spice for flavour, and plenty of sweetness from the potatoes and peas. If your family likes mushrooms, consider adding a packet of quartered ordinary mushrooms for an added vegetable. A lovely, warming dish.

Serves: 2 adults + 2 children
Prep: 10 minutes
Cook: 30 minutes

500g sweet potatoes, peeled
   and cut into 1cm cubes
4 banana shallots, peeled
   and quartered
2 teaspoons ground cumin
1 teaspoon ground coriander
$\frac{1}{2}$ teaspoon ground turmeric
2 tablespoons oil
1 teaspoon sea salt flakes
   (optional)
1 x 400g tin of coconut milk
300ml boiling water
150g frozen peas, defrosted
100g red lentils

TO SERVE
1-2 limes, juice only
A handful of fresh coriander,
   chopped

Preheat the oven to 210°C fan/230°C/gas 8. Put everything into the roasting tin, except the coconut milk, water, peas and lentils. Mix, then roast for 5 minutes. Add the coconut milk, water, peas and lentils, stir well and cook for a further 25 minutes, until the potatoes are cooked through.

Be careful opening the oven, as this dish will release quite a lot of steam. Once cooked, taste and adjust with lime juice and salt as needed, scatter over the fresh coriander and serve hot with rice or flatbreads.

CHANGE IT UP: For adults, add 1 teaspoon of chilli powder when you roast the sweet potatoes, or finely chopped fresh red chilli at the end.

ROASTED BROCCOLI & BACON CONCHIGLIE BAKE WITH LEMON CRÈME FRAÎCHE

I like to make this mac & cheese-style dish in a large, shallow roasting tin, so you get the maximum surface area for the crunchy topping. There's broccoli and spinach for added greens and a wonderful savoury note from the bacon. Feel free to use any cheese you have left over in the fridge; blue cheese or cheddar would work well.

Serves: 2 adults + 2 children
Prep: 10 minutes
Cook: 25–30 minutes

300g conchiglie or other
  favourite pasta shape
1 large head of broccoli,
  chopped into small bits
  (the size of rough granola)
160g free-range bacon lardons
A few sprigs of fresh thyme
3 tablespoons olive oil
400g crème fraîche
100g spinach, roughly chopped
1/2 a lemon, juice only
1 teaspoon sea salt (optional)
30g parmesan cheese, grated
40g panko or fresh white
breadcrumbs

Preheat the oven to 200°C fan/220°C/gas 7. Cook the conchiglie in boiling salted water for 10 minutes, then drain. While the pasta is cooking, tip the broccoli, bacon and thyme into a large roasting tin, mix with 1 tablespoon of the olive oil, then transfer to the oven and roast for 10 minutes while the pasta cooks.

Stir the cooked, drained pasta through the roasted broccoli and bacon, along with another tablespoon of oil, the crème fraîche, spinach, lemon juice and sea salt (if using).

Scatter the dish with the parmesan and breadcrumbs, drizzle with the remaining tablespoon of oil, then bake for a further 15–20 minutes, until the top is golden brown and crunchy. Serve hot.

MAKE IT VEGGIE: Consider substituting the bacon with a jar of sliced artichokes, drained and chopped into slightly smaller bits, and use vegetarian parmesan.

SIMPLE ROASTED PEPPER ORZOTTO

The all-in-one cherry tomato and bay orzo from *The Green Roasting Tin* was such a popular recipe that it got me thinking about other very simple baked orzo toppings. In this dish, the sweet roasted peppers work beautifully with the rosemary and pasta for a quick, filling weeknight dinner. Leftovers are great for lunchboxes too.

Serves: 2 adults + 2 children
Prep: 10 minutes
Cook: 25 minutes

300g orzo
600ml vegetable stock
3 peppers (red, yellow, orange), finely sliced
1 red onion, finely chopped
2–3 sprigs of fresh rosemary, leaves finely chopped
1 teaspoon sea salt flakes (optional)
2 tablespoons olive oil
1 lemon, zest and juice
Freshly ground black pepper
A handful of flaked toasted almonds
A handful of fresh basil leaves, torn

Preheat the oven to 180°C fan/200°C/gas 6. Tip the orzo and stock into a roasting tin. On your chopping board (or in a bowl if not quite enough room) mix the peppers and onion with the rosemary, sea salt (if using) and 1 tablespoon of olive oil, then scatter this in an even layer over the orzo and stock.

Transfer to the oven and cook for 25 minutes, until the peppers are lightly roasted and the orzo is cooked through.

Stir in the lemon juice and zest, another tablespoon of olive oil and a good grind of black pepper, then taste and check the seasoning: you may wish to add more salt or lemon juice. Scatter with the flaked toasted almonds and fresh basil before serving.

CHANGE IT UP: If you aren't vegan, you can add a handful of crumbled feta or goat's cheese to the dish, but it's lovely as it is.

QUICK COOK CAULIFLOWER CHEESE
WITH CRÈME FRAÎCHE, MUSTARD & KALE

I love cauliflower cheese but am not always minded to make a bechamel sauce. This version with mutard and kale is a real crowd-pleaser. The two cheeses are to my mind entirely necessary for flavour purposes.

Serves: 2
Prep: 10 minutes
Cook: 25 minutes

1 large cauliflower,
  cut into small florets
Stems and leaves from the
  cauliflower, roughly chopped
250g chopped kale
400g crème fraîche
1 free-range egg
3 heaped teaspoons Dijon
  mustard
80g cheddar cheese, grated
1 teaspoon sea salt flakes
  (optional)
200g feta cheese, crumbled
50g panko or white breadcrumbs
Freshly ground black pepper
1 tablespoon olive oil
Toasted baguette slices, to serve

Preheat the oven to 200°C fan/220°C/gas 7. Pop the cauliflower florets, stems, leaves and kale in a large bowl, and pour over a kettleful of boiling water. Let it stand for 2 minutes, then drain the veg really well. Tip everything into a roasting tin large enough to hold the veg in a single layer.

While the cauliflower is blanching, mix the crème fraîche, egg, Dijon mustard, cheddar cheese and sea salt (if using) together. Stir this through the veg in the roasting tin, then top with the crumbled feta, breadcrumbs and freshly ground black pepper. Drizzle with the olive oil, then transfer to the oven and roast for 25 minutes, until golden brown and crisp on top.

Let it sit for 5 minutes, then serve hot with some toasted baguette slices on the side.

CHANGE IT UP: If you're all out of kale, use finely chopped spring greens or cavolo nero instead. And if you're not veggie, you could add a handful of chopped chorizo, pancetta or free-range bacon lardons to the topping.

ALL-IN-ONE NIGELLA-SPICED WHOLE TOMATO DHAL

In this simple one-pot dhal, the cumin-spiced onion softens while the dhal cooks and infuses with the whole cherry tomatoes and their vines – hands free and completely delicious. You could add a couple of tablespoons of coconut cream at the end for richness if you wish, but it is perfect as it is with flatbreads or buttery basmati rice.

Serves: 4
Prep: 10 minutes
Cook: 30 minutes

400g cherry tomatoes on
  the vine
140g red lentils, rinsed
3 teaspoons nigella (black onion)
  seeds
500ml boiling water
1 teaspoon sea salt flakes
  (optional)
1 onion, finely sliced
2 teaspoons ground cumin
1 teaspoon ground coriander
1 tablespoon olive or vegetable oil
1 lemon, juice only
Flatbreads or basmati rice
  to serve

Preheat the oven to 200°C fan/220°C/gas 7. Tip the cherry tomatoes and their vines into a small lidded casserole dish or roasting tin (I separate these to make the vines easier to fish out at the end), then add the lentils, nigella seeds, boiling water and salt (if using). Prod with a spoon to make sure the vines are submerged in the water.

Dress the sliced onion with the ground cumin, coriander and oil, then scatter this over the tomato and lentil mixture. Cover with a lid or tightly scrunch a double layer of foil over the tin – you want a really good seal here, or the lentils won't cook – then transfer to the oven and cook for 30 minutes.

After 30 minutes, remove the vines, then give the dhal a good whisk. Add the lemon juice and salt to taste and serve with rice or flatbreads.

NOTE: The dhal will thicken a lot as it cools down and can be made ahead and warmed up, in fact it's even better the next day.

ROASTED AUBERGINE, COURGETTE & MACARONI BAKE

This is such an easy pasta bake and a good way to get hidden vegetables into what looks like a tomato sauce. If you use a Boursin cheese instead of my usual go-to goat's cheese or feta, you get the added flavours of garlic and herbs without having to add in extra garlic or herbs, which is helpful if you're short of time.

Serves: 3–4
Prep: 10 minutes
Cook: 30 minutes

1 aubergine, cut into 1cm cubes
1 courgette, cut into 1cm cubes
1 teaspoon sea salt flakes
   (optional)
3 tablespoons olive oil
300g macaroni
2 x 400g tins of chopped
   tomatoes
1 x 150g Boursin cheese,
   crumbled into small chunks
40g panko breadcrumbs

Preheat the oven to 210°C fan/230°C/gas 8. Get a large pan of boiling salted water ready. Tip the aubergines, courgettes, sea salt (if using) and 1 tablespoon of olive oil into a large roasting tin, mix well, then transfer to the oven and roast for 10 minutes.

Meanwhile, tip the pasta into the boiling water and cook for 10 minutes. Drain well, then remove the tin with the aubergines and courgettes from the oven and stir through the pasta, tinned tomatoes and another tablespoon of oil. Reduce the oven temperature to 200°C fan/220°C/gas 7.

Scatter over the Boursin cheese, then the breadcrumbs. Drizzle everything with the remaining tablespoon of oil, then transfer to the oven and bake for a further 15–20 minutes, until crisp and golden brown. Leave to sit for 5 minutes before serving.

MAKE AHEAD LUNCHBOXES

TEN MINUTES PREP ON SUNDAY & A STACK OF PACKED LUNCHES FOR WORK

MAKE AHEAD LUNCHBOXES

CINNAMON-SPICED AUBERGINES WITH FETA CHEESE,
OLIVES & HERBED BULGUR WHEAT (V)

QUICK COOK BROCCOLI, GRUYÈRE
& PARMA HAM QUICHE

LIGHTLY ROASTED CHICKPEA, HALLOUMI
& RED ONION SALAD WITH CORIANDER &
GIANT COUS COUS (V)

ROASTED FIG, CHICORY & HAZELNUT
LUNCHBOX SALAD

GIANT COUS COUS WITH CHORIZO,
ARTICHOKES, SPINACH & LEMON

TIKKA-SPICED PANEER SALAD
WITH CHICKPEAS, MINT & NAAN CROUTONS (V)

MINI ARTICHOKE TARTS
WITH MUSHROOMS & DILL (VEGAN)

HONEY ROAST BUTTERNUT SQUASH SALAD
WITH CHICKPEAS, GOAT'S CHEESE & ROCKET (V)

ORZO GIARDINIERA: BAKED ORZO
WITH COURGETTE, CHILLI & LEMON (VEGAN)

ROASTED HALLOUMI & BULGUR WHEAT SALAD
WITH AVOCADO, MANGO & CORIANDER (V)

CINNAMON-SPICED AUBERGINES WITH FETA CHEESE, OLIVES & HERBED BULGUR WHEAT

This lunchbox salad is really something to look forward to come 1pm. The herbed bulgur is absolutely delicious with the roasted aubergines, sharp feta cheese and pops of sweetness from the pomegranate seeds. It's lovely at room temperature, or warmed through if you can.

Serves: 3 lunchboxes
Prep: 10 minutes
Cook: 25 minutes

200g bulgur wheat, rinsed
400ml vegetable stock
100g green pitted olives
1 large aubergine,
  sliced into $1/2$cm half moons
1 red onion, thickly sliced
1 scant teaspoon ground
  cinnamon
$1/2$ a nutmeg, grated
1 teaspoon sea salt flakes
2 tablespoons olive oil
25g flat-leaf parsley leaves,
  finely chopped
100g rocket, finely chopped
1 lemon, juice only, plus
  more if needed
1 tablespoon extra virgin olive oil
200g feta cheese, crumbled
1 pomegranate, seeds only

MAKE IT VEGAN: Leave out the feta cheese at the end and add a tin of drained, rinsed chickpeas with the aubergines at step 2 for some added protein.

Preheat the oven to 200°C fan/220°C/gas 7. You will need two roasting tins for this dish: trust me I've tried doing it all in just one tin, and the aubergines do not like it. Tip the bulgur wheat, vegetable stock and olives into a smaller roasting tin while you get on with slicing the aubergines and onion.

Mix the vegetables with the cinnamon, nutmeg, salt and olive oil in a second roasting tin, large enough to hold everything in a single layer. Transfer both roasting tins to the oven for 25 minutes, until the aubergines are crisp and cooked through and the bulgur wheat is fluffy, with all the stock absorbed.

Stir the greens, lemon juice and extra virgin olive oil through the bulgur wheat, then taste and adjust the salt and lemon juice as needed.

Let everything cool down, then transfer the bulgur wheat into lunchboxes, top with the roasted aubergines and scatter the feta cheese and pomegranate seeds over the top. Refrigerate until needed.

QUICK COOK BROCCOLI, GRUYÈRE & PARMA HAM QUICHE

This recipe is an adapted version of the broccoli and blue cheese puff pastry quiche from *The Green Roasting Tin*, inspired by my friend Sapphire, who told me about a version of the quiche she made with Parma ham. It works beautifully with the gruyère and sage leaves for a smart, French-style lunchbox.

Serves: 4–6 lunchboxes
Prep: 10 minutes
Cook: 25 minutes

320g ready-rolled
  puff pastry sheet
350g broccoli,
  cut into small florets
1 red onion, roughly chopped
100g crème fraîche
4 free-range eggs
75g gruyère cheese, grated
A pinch of sea salt flakes
Freshly ground black pepper
8 fresh sage leaves
140g Parma ham

Preheat the oven to 200°C fan/220°C/gas 7. Lay the puff pastry, leaving it on the paper that it comes wrapped in, in a roasting tin or baking dish, small enough that the pastry comes up the 4 sides of the dish to form a shallow 'cup' for the rest of the ingredients. Don't worry about the overhang, it'll crisp up.

Scatter the broccoli florets and red onion over the pastry. Whisk the crème fraîche, eggs and grated cheese together with a pinch of salt and freshly ground black pepper and pour this all over the vegetables.

Scatter over the sage leaves, lay the Parma ham over the top, then transfer the quiche to the oven and bake for 25 minutes, until the pastry is golden brown and the filling just set.

Let the quiche cool down a little before slicing and serving. It's excellent hot or cold.

MAKE IT VEGGIE: Leave out the Parma ham, add a few more sage leaves, substitute the gruyère with cheddar, and grate a little more cheddar over the top of the quiche before baking. (I would think about adding a few sliced mushrooms, but that's because I add mushrooms to everything.)

LIGHTLY ROASTED CHICKPEA, HALLOUMI & RED ONION SALAD WITH CORIANDER & GIANT COUS COUS

I've been making a version of this salad for years, because chickpeas, halloumi, red onion and lemon are a magic combination, with either flat-leaf parsley or coriander for a herby lift. But it's far too nice just to have as a side salad: add carbs in the form of giant cous cous and you'll have enviable lunchboxes with only 10 minutes' hands-on work.

Serves: 2–3 lunchboxes
Prep: 10 minutes
Cook: 30 minutes

200g wholewheat giant
   cous cous
400ml vegetable stock
250g halloumi,
   cut into 1cm chunks
1 x 400g tin of chickpeas,
   drained and rinsed
1 red onion, finely sliced
1 tablespoon olive oil
1 teaspoon smoked paprika
1 tablespoon extra virgin olive oil
1 tablespoon lemon juice
100g spinach, roughly chopped
15g coriander, roughly chopped
Sea salt flakes, to taste

Preheat the oven to 180°C fan/200°C/gas 6. Tip the cous cous and vegetable stock into a medium-sized roasting tin. Toss the halloumi, chickpeas and red onion with the olive oil and paprika and scatter this all over the cous cous.

Transfer the tin to the oven and bake for 25–30 minutes, until the halloumi is golden brown and the cous cous is cooked through.

Stir through the extra virgin olive oil, lemon juice and greens, then taste and adjust the seasoning as required.

Divide between lunchboxes and refrigerate until needed. Best eaten at room temperature.

ROASTED FIG, CHICORY & HAZELNUT LUNCHBOX SALAD

Honey roasted figs, chicory and hazelnuts are a beautiful base for this easy salad. Cook it in stages below for a simple yet delicious lunchbox, or eat immediately while the chikcen is still hot. It's nice enough for a dinner party.

Serves: 2 lunchboxes
Prep: 10 minutes
Cook: 25–30 minutes

2 heads of chicory, halved if small,
  quartered if big
4 figs, halved
40g blanched hazelnuts
1 red onion, roughly sliced
2 free-range chicken breasts
2 tablespoons olive oil
1 teaspoon sea salt
Freshly ground black pepper
A good drizzle of honey
2 mini rosemary focaccias,
  torn into rough pieces
100g rocket

FOR THE DRESSING
1 lemon, juice only
1 tablespoon extra virgin olive oil
A pinch of sea salt
Freshly ground black pepper

Preheat the oven to 180°C fan/200°C/gas 6. Tip the chicory, figs, hazelnuts, onion and chicken breasts into a roasting tin large enough to hold everything in a single layer. Mix gently with 1 tablespoon of the olive oil, the sea salt and freshly ground black pepper, then drizzle with the honey.

Scatter the bread over the top, then transfer the tin to the oven and cook for 25–30 minutes, until the chicken is cooked through. Meanwhile, whisk the lemon juice, extra virgin olive oil, salt and pepper for the dressing together.

Let the chicken and vegetables cool down, then slice the chicken. Divide the rocket between 2 lunchboxes, top evenly with the vegetables and sliced chicken, then refrigerate, along with the dressing, in a couple of little pots or jars. Pop the toasted focaccia into 2 airtight bags or containers to keep it crisp and mix everything together just before you eat.

MAKE IT VEGGIE: Substitute the chicken with 250g goat's cheese with a rind, cut into thick slices and baked along with the figs.

GIANT COUS COUS WITH CHORIZO, ARTICHOKES, SPINACH & LEMON

I wish I'd had this recipe when I worked in an office. It's so simple to make, a perfect balance of flavours and textures and tastes even better the next day. If you aren't a fan of chorizo (if not, why not?) or fancy a vegetarian version, see the note below: it's lovely with avocado too. There are fresh greens stirred through at the end, but we took this photograph before that, because it looked so lovely straight out of the oven.

Serves: 3 lunchboxes
Prep: 10 minutes
Cook: 20–25 minutes

200g wholewheat giant
  cous cous
400ml vegetable stock
200g jarred artichokes, drained
1 red onion, roughly sliced
80–100g diced chorizo, finely
  chopped
150g spinach, finely chopped
1 lemon, zest and juice
Sea salt flakes
Freshly ground black pepper

Preheat the oven to 180°C fan/200°C/gas 6. Tip the cous cous, stock, jarred artichokes and onion into a roasting tin, and scatter over the chopped chorizo. Cover the tin tightly with foil, then transfer to the oven and bake for 20–25 minutes.

Once cooked, stir through the spinach and the lemon zest and juice. (You shouldn't need to add extra oil, as there's enough released by the chorizo and artichokes.) Taste and season with the sea salt and black pepper as needed.

Let everything cool down before dividing into lunchboxes. Refrigerate until needed.

MAKE IT VEGAN: Leave out the chorizo and add 1 heaped teaspoon of smoked paprika. Dress with 1 big tablespoon of oil from the artichoke jar once it's finished cooking and serve with a freshly sliced avocado (don't slice it until you're ready to eat, or it will discolour).

TIKKA-SPICED PANEER SALAD WITH CHICKPEAS, MINT & NAAN CROUTONS

Naan croutons might be the best crouton ever invented (I would happily eat a trayful) and they work beautifully here in this Indian-inspired take on an Italian panzanella salad. Try to find plain naan bread with nigella (black onion) seeds, as they have a wonderful flavour. You can find good shop-bought paneer in the cheese section of the supermarket, it roasts beautifully with the spices.

Serves: 4 generous lunchboxes
Prep: 10 minutes
Cook: 25–30 minutes

2 x 225g packets of paneer, cut
    or broken into 2$\frac{1}{2}$cm chunks
1 x 400g tin of chickpeas,
    drained and rinsed
1 red onion, roughly sliced
1 clove of garlic, finely grated
2$\frac{1}{2}$cm fresh ginger, grated
1 teaspoon ground turmeric
1 teaspoon ground cumin
$\frac{1}{2}$ teaspoon mild chilli powder
1 teaspoon smoked paprika
1 teaspoon sea salt flakes
50g natural yogurt
2 tablespoons olive oil
2 naan breads, cut or torn
    into 2$\frac{1}{2}$cm pieces

TO SERVE
1 bag of watercress (85-100g),
    roughly chopped
A large handful of fresh mint
    leaves, roughly chopped
1 lemon, juice only
1 tablespoon olive oil
Natural yogurt

Preheat the oven to 180°C fan/200°C/gas 6. Tip the paneer chunks into a large roasting tin along with the chickpeas, red onion, garlic, ginger, spices, salt, yogurt and 1 tablespoon of olive oil, and mix really well until everything is evenly coated.

Toss the naan bread pieces with the remaining 1 tablespoon of olive oil and pop these into a separate baking tray or tin.

Transfer the tins to the oven and roast for 25–30 minutes, until the naan bread is crisp and the paneer is just charring at the edges.

Let the roasted paneer cool down, then stir through the chopped watercress and mint along with the lemon juice and oil. Taste and adjust the salt as needed.

Pack the yogurt and crispy naan croutons separately and stir the croutons through the salad just before eating with the yogurt.

CHANGE IT UP: If you aren't veggie, you can adapt this salad really easily using 500g of chopped chicken breast instead of the paneer.

MINI ARTICHOKE TARTS
WITH MUSHROOMS & DILL

Ordinary shop-bought puff pastry is almost always vegan – who knew? I didn't until recently, but it's a revelation. These easy little vegan tarts with a filling of mushrooms and artichokes are perfect for lunchboxes or picnics and only need a bit of salad on the side.

Serves: 4 lunchboxes
Prep: 10 minutes
Cook: 25 minutes

1 x 320g ready-rolled vegan
   puff pastry sheet
2 teaspoons mustard
200g chestnut mushrooms,
   finely sliced
1 x 240g jarred sliced artichokes
   drained, halved to $1/2$ cm thick
1 lemon, juice only
A few sprigs of fresh dill,
   roughly chopped
Sea salt flakes

Preheat the oven to 180°C fan/200°C/gas 6. Line a baking tray with greaseproof paper, then cut the pastry into 8 pieces and space them evenly on the tray. Spread a little mustard over each pastry square, leaving a 1cm border.

Arrange the mushrooms on top of the mustard on each tart – don't panic if looks like there's an absolute mountain of mushrooms on each one – they'll shrink so much on cooking. Arrange the sliced artichokes on top like little spooning penguins, then transfer to the oven and roast for 25 minutes, until golden brown. (There's enough oil on the artichokes that you don't need to add extra oil to the mushrooms.)

Once cooked, squeeze the lemon juice over the artichokes, then scatter each tart with dill and a pinch of sea salt before serving, or cool and refrigerate until needed.

HONEY ROAST BUTTERNUT SQUASH SALAD WITH CHICKPEAS, GOAT'S CHEESE & ROCKET

This is a delicious lunchbox salad, but it'd also definitely be nice enough to make for friends as part of a sharing dinner. Cumin works wonders with the squash and the lemon dressing lifts the salad at the end. It's extremely moreish.

Serves: 4 lunchboxes
Prep: 10 minutes
Cook: 30 minutes

1kg butternut squash, peeled
    and cut into 1cm cubes
    (or use ready-cubed squash,
    and cut the cubes smaller)
1 x 400g tin of chickpeas,
    rinsed and drained
1 red onion, roughly sliced
2 cloves of garlic, crushed
1 tablespoon olive oil
1 heaped teaspoon ground cumin
1 teaspoon sea salt flakes
1 tablespoon honey

FOR THE DRESSING
1 lemon, juice only
1 tablespoon extra virgin olive oil
Freshly ground black pepper

TO SERVE
100g rocket, roughly chopped
125g goat's cheese, crumbled

Preheat the oven to 200°C fan/220°C/gas 7. Tip the squash, chickpeas and onion into a roasting tin large enough for everything to sit in a single layer (you may want to use the shelf that comes fitted in the oven). Mix through the crushed garlic, olive oil, cumin and sea salt, drizzle over the honey, then transfer to the oven and roast for 30 minutes.

Meanwhile, whisk the lemon juice, extra virgin olive oil and black pepper together.

Once the squash is cooked, stir through the dressing and the rocket and top with the crumbled goat's cheese.

CARB IT UP: For a carbed-up salad, pop 200g bulgur wheat or orzo into the tin along with 400ml vegetable stock. Dress the veg in another bowl or tin before scattering it over the grains and stock, then bake as above. Taste and adjust the olive oil, lemon juice and salt at the end to account for the extra ingredients.

ORZO GIARDINIERA: BAKED ORZO WITH COURGETTE, CHILLI & LEMON

I thought it wasn't possible to improve on the texture of baked orzo – yet this dish has proved me happily wrong. The courgette melts into the most incredibly rich, creamy sauce for the pasta, pepped up with some fresh chilli and pine nuts for crunch. This is sure to become a lunchbox favourite. I've been known to pop a half portion of it in the oven before breakfast, and lunch is ready to take out with me within half an hour.

Serves: 2–3 lunchboxes
Prep: 10 minutes
Cook: 20–25 minutes

200g orzo
2 large courgettes, grated
1 tablespoon olive oil
400ml vegetable stock
100g spinach, chopped
1 lemon, juice only
1 red chilli, deseeded
   and finely chopped
50g toasted pine nuts

Preheat the oven to 180°C fan/200°C/gas 6. Tip the orzo into a roasting tin and scatter over the grated courgettes. Pour over the oil and vegetable stock, transfer to the oven and bake for 20–25 minutes.

Once the orzo is cooked, stir through the spinach and lemon juice, then top with the red chilli and toasted pine nuts.

If you're making this ahead for lunchboxes, consider adding a handful of halved fresh cherry tomatoes. The dish reheats well in the microwave.

MAKE IT VEGGIE: You can scatter over some crumbled feta cheese for a vegetarian version.

ROASTED HALLOUMI & BULGUR WHEAT SALAD WITH AVOCADO, MANGO & CORIANDER

This is everything I want for a make-ahead meal: minimum effort on a Sunday, followed by a couple of days of colourful, tasty lunchboxes. Halloumi works so well with mango for a blend of sweet and savoury and there's a fresh green hit from the spinach and coriander. Definitely pop it into the microwave at work, though, as the cheese tastes best when hot.

Serves: 3 generous lunchboxes
Prep: 10 minutes
Cook: 25 minutes

200g bulgur wheat, rinsed
400ml vegetable stock
1 red onion, roughly sliced
250g halloumi,
 cut into $1\frac{1}{2}$ cm chunks
1 tablespoon extra virgin olive oil
1 lime, juice only (use 2 if it's
 not very juicy)
A big handful of fresh coriander,
 roughly chopped
A couple of handfuls of spinach,
 roughly chopped
1 firm mango, finely sliced
Freshly ground black pepper
1 small firm avocado per serving

Preheat the oven to 180°C fan/200°C/gas 6. Mix the bulgur wheat and vegetable stock in a roasting tin, then top with the red onion and halloumi. Transfer to the oven and roast for 25 minutes, until the halloumi is golden brown and crisp on top.

Stir through the extra virgin olive oil, lime juice, coriander, spinach, mango and freshly ground black pepper. Taste and adjust the seasoning as needed, then pack into lunchboxes. Take the avocado with you and slice it into the salad after you've warmed it up and just before you eat it.

DATE NIGHT

MAXIMUM IMPACT,
SERIOUSLY LOW-EFFORT
DINNERS TO IMPRESS

DATE NIGHT

THYME ROASTED RICOTTA WITH VINE TOMATOES,
BABY AUBERGINES & RED ONION (V)

CREAMY BAKED GNOCCHI WITH DOLCELATTE,
FIGS & HAZELNUT (V)

SCALLOP, LEEK & CHORIZO GRATIN

SAGE & WILD MUSHROOM TART (VEGAN)

PISTACHIO CRUSTED LAMB
WITH ROASTED HERBED VEG

VIETNAMESE-STYLE FISH WITH TURMERIC,
SPRING ONIONS & DILL

POMEGRANATE DUCK WITH WALNUTS
& RAINBOW TABBOULEH

PINE NUT CRUSTED SALMON
WITH SHALLOTS & PUY LENTILS

ASPARAGUS, POMEGRANATE & PINE NUT
TARTS (VEGAN)

ROSEMARY & HAZELNUT ROASTED COD
WITH TOMATOES & HERBED SPELT

THYME ROASTED RICOTTA WITH VINE TOMATOES, BABY AUBERGINES & RED ONION

Think of this as like a home-made antipasti platter – the flavours from the herbs and just-charred vegetables work beautifully with the whole roasted ricotta. As with other very simple dishes, the quality of the ricotta is important, so buy the nicest you can find.

Serves: 2
Prep: 10 minutes
Cook: 20 minutes

5 baby aubergines, cut into thirds (or ordinary aubergines, halved and very finely sliced)
250g cherry tomatoes on the vine
1 red onion, roughly chopped
2 tablespoons olive oil
1 teaspoon sea salt flakes
7–8 sprigs of fresh thyme
2–3 sprigs of fresh rosemary
5–6 fresh sage leaves
1 x 250g whole ricotta
1 tablespoon extra virgin olive oil
$\frac{1}{2}$ a lemon, zest and juice
Good sliced focaccia or olive bread, to serve

Preheat the oven to 200°C fan/220°C/gas 7. Mix the aubergines, tomatoes, their vines and the onion in a roasting tin with 1 tablespoon of the oil, the sea salt and half the herbs. Move the vegetables to leave space for the ricotta in the centre, then upend the ricotta from its tub into the gap.

Drizzle the ricotta with the remaining oil, scatter everything including the ricotta with the rest of the herbs and another pinch of salt, then transfer to the oven and bake for 20 minutes. Meanwhile, whisk the extra virgin olive oil and lemon zest and juice together.

After 20 minutes, the vegetables should be cooked through and nicely charred. Take the tin out of the oven, dress everything with the oil and lemon mixture, scatter a good pinch of salt over everything and serve with some really good focaccia or olive bread.

CREAMY BAKED GNOCCHI WITH DOLCELATTE, FIGS & HAZELNUT

This is just such a wonderful dish, the combination of hot blue cheese, figs and hazelnuts is incredible against the gnocchi. It will bubble furiously as you take it out of the oven, so give it five minutes or so to cool down before you dive in.

Serves: 2
Prep: 10 minutes
Cook: 30 minutes

400g gnocchi
2 heaped tablespoons
  crème fraîche (about 100g)
1 teaspoon sea salt
Freshly ground black pepper
150g dolcelatte, roughly torn
4 figs, quartered
Runny honey
40g hazelnuts, roughly chopped

TO SERVE
85g watercress
1 tablespoon lemon juice
$\frac{1}{2}$ tablespoon extra virgin
  olive oil

Preheat the oven to 180°C fan/200°C/gas 6. Put the gnocchi into a large bowl, pour over a kettleful of boiling water and leave it to sit for 2 minutes.

Drain the gnocchi well, tip it into a roasting tin large enough to hold it all snugly in a single layer, then stir through the crème fraîche. Season with salt and some freshly ground black pepper.

Scatter over the torn dolcelatte and quartered figs, then squeeze the barest drop of honey on to each fig quarter: it'll improve the flavour no end. (If you don't have a squeezy bottle, use a spoon to put tiny drops on instead.) Scatter with the hazelnuts, then transfer to the oven and bake for 30 minutes.

Once the gnocchi has had 30 minutes, dress the watercress with the lemon juice and extra virgin olive oil. Scatter a few watercress leaves over the top of the gnocchi just before serving and serve the rest of the salad alongside.

SCALLOP, LEEK & CHORIZO GRATIN

This is a lovely, easy way to prepare scallops, which work beautifully with the punchy chorizo and creamy leeks. If you have little individual ceramic dishes, by all means use those for smart presentation. Though if your date isn't impressed by a giant dish of crunchy-topped gratin brought to the table as it is, you may wish to rethink your dinner companion.

Serves: 2 generously
Prep: 10 minutes
Cook: 20–25 minutes

1 large or 2 small leeks, halved and finely sliced
1 teaspoon sea salt flakes
Freshly ground black pepper
300g scallops, sliced in half if very large
75g chorizo, finely chopped
250ml double cream
A big handful (about 10g) of fresh flat-leaf parsley leaves, finely chopped
50g panko breadcrumbs
30g grated parmesan
$\frac{1}{2}$ a lemon, zest only
1 tablespoon olive oil
Really good bread and butter, to serve (think fresh baguette or sourdough)

Preheat the oven to 180°C fan/200°C/gas 6. Pop the sliced leeks into a bowl and pour over a kettleful of boiling water. Leave them to sit for 2 minutes, then drain well and tip into a medium-sized roasting tin or ceramic lasagne dish. Season with the sea salt and a good grind of black pepper.

Arrange the scallops over the leeks, then scatter over the chorizo and pour the double cream evenly over everything.

Mix the finely chopped parsley with the panko breadcrumbs, parmesan and lemon zest, then scatter this over the dish. Drizzle over the olive oil, then transfer to the oven to bake for 20–25 minutes, until the topping is golden brown and crunchy and the scallops cooked through.

Leave it to cool down for 5 minutes, before serving hot with the bread and butter.

SAGE & WILD MUSHROOM TART

This is a wonderfully rich, filling dish. It certainly makes more than enough for two, but looks like such an impressive centrepiece and tastes so lovely that I just had to include it in the date night section. There is a little bit of work blitzing the nuts and herbs for the vegan base, but it is otherwise an easy dish to accomplish.

Serves: 2 generously
Prep: 10 minutes
Cook: 25 minutes

200g pine nuts
20g flat-leaf parsley
175ml water
15ml lemon juice
2 teaspoons sea salt flakes
1 tablespoon olive oil, plus more
    for the tin and the filo
4 sheets of filo pastry (check the
    packet to ensure it is vegan)
200g chestnut mushrooms,
    halved
100g wild mushrooms,
    halved if large
10 sage leaves, finely chopped
2 sprigs of rosemary, leaves
    finely chopped

TO SERVE
1 lemon, juice only
Sea salt flakes
A little finely chopped
    flat-leaf parsley leaves
Freshly ground black pepper

Preheat the oven to 180°C fan/200°C/gas 6. Blitz the pine nuts, parsley, water, lemon juice and 1 teaspoon of sea salt flakes in a high-speed blender until you have a thick, smooth green paste. It should look like very thick green hummus. Set aside.

Oil and line a 24–25cm pie dish or small roasting tin with baking paper. Lay over a sheet of filo pastry, brush it with oil, then lay another on it at a 90° angle. You'll have a lot of overhang, but don't worry about this yet. Repeat, so you have 4 layers of oiled pastry, then fold the overhang back to form the tart edges, scrumpling it a little if you wish.

Spread the pine nut mixture over the pastry base. Toss the mushrooms with the chopped sage, rosemary, oil and another teaspoon of sea salt, then scatter them evenly over the tart. Transfer to the oven and bake for 25 minutes, until the pastry is golden brown.

Squeeze over the lemon juice, scatter over a pinch of sea salt flakes and a little flat-leaf parsley, grind over a generous amount of black pepper, and serve with a light lemon-dressed spinach salad (see page 30).

PISTACHIO CRUSTED LAMB WITH ROASTED HERBED VEG

This is such a lovely dish for a special occasion. A French-trimmed rack of lamb is a little more pricey than other cuts, but all the meat is meltingly tender and it looks really impressive compared to how easy it is to prepare. If you can get multi-coloured carrots, this is the time to deploy them. See page 218 for tips on plating up.

Serves: 2
Prep: 10 minutes
Cook: 20–30 minutes

150g baby carrots,
    halved lengthways
200g baby courgettes,
    halved lengthways
1 x 400g tin of haricot beans,
    drained and rinsed
1 tablespoon olive oil
2 teaspoons sea salt flakes
Freshly ground black pepper
1 x approx. 350g French-trimmed
    rack of lamb
2 teaspoons Dijon mustard
40g pistachio nuts, fairly finely
    chopped
1 small bunch of fresh mint,
    leaves finely chopped
$\frac{1}{2}$ a lemon, juice only
1 tablespoon extra virgin olive oil

Preheat the oven to 180°C fan/200°C/gas 6. Tip the vegetables, beans, olive oil, 1 teaspoon of sea salt and a good grind of black pepper into a roasting tin and mix well.

Rub the rack of lamb with the remaining teaspoon of sea salt, then lay it on top of the vegetables and spread the top and sides with the mustard. Scatter the pistachios evenly over the top and gently press them down.

Transfer the tin to the oven and cook for 20–30 minutes depending on whether you prefer lamb rare or well done (I like 25 minutes).

Remove the tin from the oven, and put the lamb on to a board to rest for 10 minutes. This is really important for the texture, so don't skip it. Meanwhile, dress the vegetables with the mint, lemon juice and extra virgin olive oil, then taste and adjust the seasoning as needed.

Once the lamb has rested, use a sharp knife to slice it into neat medallions (do this at a slight angle to cut between the bones) and arrange them over the vegetables in the tin. Pour any juices from the chopping board over the lamb, then serve immediately.

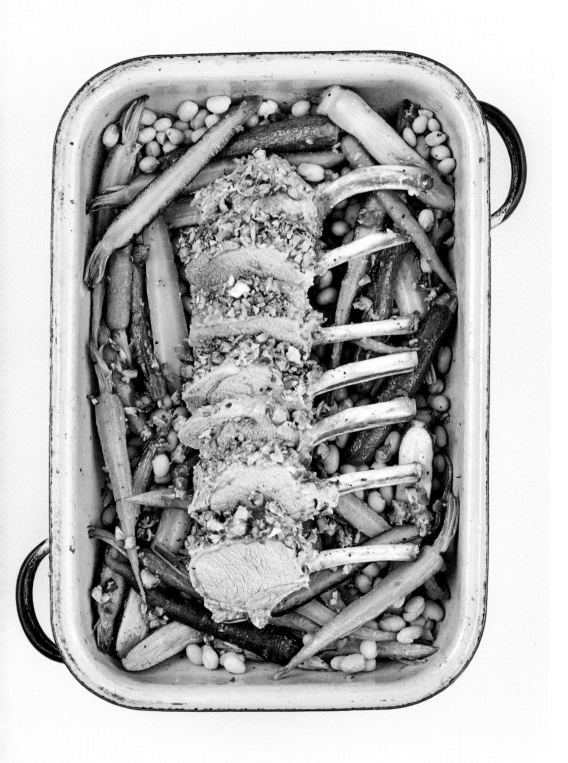

VIETNAMESE-STYLE FISH WITH TURMERIC, SPRING ONIONS & DILL

This is an oven version of the famous Vietnamese dish cha ca, which I first had in Hanoi with my friend Mo, in a restaurant so dedicated to the dish that it is the only thing on the menu. (Cha Ca La Vong – do go if you're visiting.) The waiters cook the fish for you then and there at the table and you have a pile of herbs, chilli and peanuts to add to your plate. It's absolutely delicious.

Serves: 2
Prep: 10 minutes
Cook: 20 minutes

300g pak choi, quartered
5 spring onions, cut diagonally
  into 1cm slices
1$\frac{1}{2}$ tablespoons oil
1 teaspoon ground turmeric
1$\frac{1}{2}$ tablespoons fish sauce
A pinch of sea salt
1 clove of garlic, crushed
1cm fresh ginger, grated
300g hake, cod or other firm
  white-fleshed fish
25g fresh dill, chopped
2 tablespoons lime juice
1 tablespoon water
$\frac{1}{2}$ teaspoon caster sugar

TO SERVE
A handful of fresh coriander,
  roughly chopped
1 red chilli, finely sliced
A handful of unsalted peanuts,
  roughly chopped
Cooked vermicelli noodles or rice

Preheat the oven to 180°C fan/200°C/gas 6. Tip the pak choi and spring onions into a roasting tin large enough to hold the veg and the fish in a single layer, and mix with $\frac{1}{2}$ tablespoon of the oil.

Mix the remaining 1 tablespoon of oil with the turmeric, $\frac{1}{2}$ tablespoon of the fish sauce, a pinch of sea salt, the garlic and ginger and use this mixture to coat the fish. Gently lay the fish over the vegetables and pour any extra mixture over the veg

Scatter the dill thickly over the fish, then transfer to the oven and bake for 20 minutes, until the fish is just cooked through.

While the fish and veg is cooking, mix the lime juice, remaining 1 tablespoon fish sauce, the water and sugar together. Pour the dressing over the cooked fish and vegetables, scatter everything with the coriander, chilli and peanuts and serve with vermicelli rice noodles or rice.

POMEGRANATE DUCK WITH WALNUTS & RAINBOW TABBOULEH

This is a really elegant little dinner, pomegranate molasses and duck are an absolutely wonderful combination. Fans of Persian cookery will recognise the combination from the classic slow-cooked pomegranate, duck and walnut fesenjan stew. This version uses quicker-cooking duck breasts, along with a moreish, herby tabbouleh for an easy date night dinner.

Serves: 2 generously
Prep: 10 minutes
Cook: 25–30 minutes

100g bulgur wheat, rinsed
200ml vegetable or chicken stock
2$\frac{1}{2}$cm fresh ginger, grated
1 fresh beetroot, peeled and
 grated
Beetroot stems and leaves,
 finely chopped
1 leek, finely sliced
1 tablespoon olive oil
2 duck breasts, skin removed
1 teaspoon sea salt flakes
60g walnuts, finely chopped
2 tablespoons pomegranate
 molasses, plus more to serve
25g fresh flat-leaf parsley leaves,
 finely chopped (reserve some
 to serve)
1 pomegranate, seeds only
1 x 100g bag of spinach,
 roughly chopped
25g fresh mint leaves, finely
 chopped (reserve a few small
 leaves to serve)
1 lime, zest and juice
1 tablespoon extra virgin olive oil

Preheat the oven to 180°C fan/200°C/gas 6. Tip the bulgur, stock and ginger into a medium-sized roasting tin, then scatter over the grated beetroot, the chopped stems and leaves and the sliced leek. Drizzle with the olive oil.

Season the duck breasts all over with the sea salt and pop them into the tin on top of the leeks. Stir the walnuts, pomegranate molasses and 1 tablespoon of the parsley together, then pat this mixture evenly over both.

Transfer to the oven and cook for 25–30 minutes, until the duck is cooked through to your liking.

Remove the duck from the tin and let it rest on a board for at least 5 minutes (this is really important for texture) while you stir half the pomegranate seeds, the rest of the parsley, the spinach, mint, lime zest and juice and extra virgin olive oil through the bulgur. Taste and adjust the salt and lime juice as needed.

To plate, slice the duck breasts and arrange them over the tabbouleh. Scatter with the remaining pomegranate seeds and the reserved parsley and mint before serving, along with a drizzle of pomegranate molasses.

PINE NUT CRUSTED SALMON WITH SHALLOTS & PUY LENTILS

I'm not sure you could do better than this for a date night dinner. It's almost zero effort, but tastes and looks restaurant quality. Because it's quite a simple dish, with just the mustard and pine nuts to flavour the salmon, this is a dish where it's worth buying the best salmon you can.

Serves: 2
Prep: 10 minutes
Cook: 20–25 minutes

4 banana/long pointy shallots, peeled and halved lengthways if small, quartered if big
1 tablespoon olive oil
1 teaspoon sea salt
2 really nice salmon fillets
2 teaspoons Dijon mustard
25g pine nuts, fairly finely chopped
A handful of flat-leaf parsley leaves, finely chopped
1 x 250g vac-pac of cooked Puy lentils
1 bag of watercress (around 80g), roughly chopped
1 tablespoon extra virgin olive oil
1 lemon, juice only
2 tablespoons single cream (optional)
Freshly ground black pepper

Preheat the oven to 180°C fan/200°C/gas 6. Mix the shallots with the olive oil and sea salt in a roasting tin, making sure the shallots are arranged cut sides facing upwards, then put the salmon steaks alongside.

Spread the top of the salmon fillets with the mustard. Mix the chopped pine nuts and parsley together (I sometimes just do this on the chopping board), then press the mixture over the mustard.

Transfer the tin to the oven and cook for 20–25 minutes, until the salmon is just cooked through (thicker pieces will take 25 minutes, thinner 20).

Remove the salmon fillets from the tin, then mix the Puy lentils, watercress, extra virgin olive oil and half the lemon juice through the shallots. Stir in the single cream, if using, then taste and adjust the lemon juice, salt and pepper as needed. Serve alongside the salmon.

NOTE: This is a dish where it's worth thinking about warming your plates through. See the note on plating on page 218.

ROSEMARY & HAZELNUT ROASTED COD WITH TOMATOES & HERBED SPELT

In this dish, the fish gently cooks as the butter from the rosemary and hazelnut crust melts through it: aka the best way to cook fish. Do use nice thick cod fillets because, if they're too small, they'll overcook in the 25 minutes it takes for the quick cook farro or spelt to cook. Alternatively, use nice big salmon steaks.

Serves: 2
Prep: 10 minutes
Cook: 25 minutes

150g quick cook farro
  or quick cook spelt
350ml boiling vegetable stock
300g cherry tomatoes on
  the vine
4 shallots, halved
40g hazelnuts, finely chopped
2 sprigs of fresh rosemary, leaves
  finely chopped
30g unsalted butter, softened
1 teaspoon sea salt
2 large thick cod fillets
150g jarred artichokes,
  oil drained and reserved
100g rocket, roughly chopped
1 lemon, juice only

Preheat the oven to 160°C fan/180°C/gas 4. Tip the farro or spelt and stock into a large roasting tin, then lay over the cherry tomatoes with their vines and the halved shallots.

Mix the hazelnuts, rosemary, softened butter and sea salt (use less sea salt if using salted butter) and spread this mixture gently over the cod fillets. Place them on top of the vegetables in the tin, cover the tin tightly with foil, then transfer to the oven and cook for 25 minutes, until the spelt is cooked but al dente and the fish is cooked through.

Remove the cod fillets from the tin and stir the artichokes, rocket and lemon juice into the spelt. Add a little extra oil from the jarred artichokes if needed, then taste and adjust the seasoning. Serve alongside the cod.

ASPARAGUS, POMEGRANATE & PINE NUT TARTS

Asparagus and buttery pine nuts are a wonderful combination and, with the pops of sweetness from the pomegranate, they work beautifully in these easy yet showstopping tarts. Bought puff pastry (in a green box) is helpfully vegan-friendly, though this dish is so nice I'd make it for non-vegans too.

Serves: 2
Prep: 10 minutes
Cook: 25 minutes

1 x 320g ready-rolled vegan
   puff pastry sheet
3 heaped tablespoons vegan
   green pesto
125g asparagus spears (often
   sold as 'asparagus tips')
$\frac{1}{2}$ tablespoon olive oil
$\frac{1}{2}$ teaspoon sea salt flakes
4 tablespoons chopped
   pine nuts
$\frac{1}{2}$ a pomegranate, seeds only
$\frac{1}{2}$ a lemon, juice only
Lemon-dressed spinach salad
   (see page 30)

Preheat the oven to 180°C fan/200°C/gas 6. Cut 2 rectangles of puff pastry the right length and width to hold your asparagus spears with a 1$\frac{1}{2}$cm border on each side, as opposite. (You will have a fair bit of leftover pastry, see the note below for ideas on what to do with it.)

Spread your 2 pastry rectangles with the vegan pesto, leaving that 1 $\frac{1}{2}$ cm border, then lay the asparagus over the top. Brush the spears with the olive oil, scatter over the sea salt, then cover thickly with a blanket of chopped pine nuts.

Transfer to the oven and bake for 25 minutes, until the pastry is golden brown and risen. Scatter over the pomegranate seeds, squeeze over the lemon juice and serve with the spinach salad alongside.

NOTE: Things to do with leftover puff pastry: cut into small rectangles, roll up with chopped dark chocolate inside and bake as mini pain au chocolat. Cut into small squares, add a spoonful of jam, then pinch together for jam puffs. Or follow Laura Goodman's recipe for lime pickle cheese straws from her fabulous book *Carbs*.

FEED A CROWD

FROM DINNER PARTIES WITH
FRIENDS TO LAZY WEEKEND
FEASTS – DOUBLE UP WITH
TWO TINS OR MIX AND MATCH

FEED A CROWD

ROASTED NECTARINES WITH GOAT'S CHEESE,
ALMONDS, WATERCRESS & CROUTONS (V)

BAKED FETA CHEESE WITH FIGS, PINE NUTS & BASIL (V)

ROSEMARY & GARLIC ROASTED LAMB
WITH ARTICHOKES & OLIVES

SESAME & THYME ROASTED CAULIFLOWER PILAF
WITH FETA CHEESE & WATERCRESS (V)

SICHUAN PEPPERED PORK CHOPS WITH APPLES & CABBAGE

ROASTED HALLOUMI WITH AUBERGINES,
TOMATOES & PINE NUTS (V)

TANDOORI-STYLE SALMON WITH SPICED, ROASTED
SWEET POTATOES, TOMATOES & RED ONION

SPICED LAMB MEATBALLS WITH SUMAC ROASTED
CAULIFLOWER & POMEGRANATE

CHARRED TENDERSTEM WITH BLACK BEANS,
AVOCADO & PEANUTS (VEGAN)

MASALA ROASTED CORN WITH QUICK CORIANDER
CHUTNEY (VEGAN)

SPICED ROAST CHICKEN WITH PEPPERS,
AUBERGINE & ONION

ROAST SWEET POTATO WITH OREGANO,
FETA CHEESE & CHARRED LEMON (V)

ROASTED NECTARINES WITH GOAT'S CHEESE, ALMONDS, WATERCRESS & CROUTONS

This is one of the nicest dinner-party starters I can think of, the nectarines and goat's cheese work perfectly with the roasted almonds and sweet, sticky balsamic dressing. You could also use peaches – or even flat peaches – when in season. (If your nectarines are on the unripe side of ready, don't panic, they'll soften up in the oven. Don't use very ripe fruit, they'll turn to mush.)

Serves: 4 as a starter
Prep: 10 minutes
Cook: 25–30 minutes

4 just-under to just-ripe
   nectarines, quartered
100g whole blanched almonds
2 sprigs of fresh rosemary,
   leaves finely chopped
1 tablespoon honey
150g rosemary focaccia,
   torn into chunks
1 tablespoon olive oil
100g watercress
125g goat's cheese log with
   a rind, sliced

FOR THE DRESSING
1 tablespoon extra virgin olive oil
2 tablespoons honey
1 tablespoon balsamic vinegar

Preheat the oven to 180°C fan/200°C/gas 6. Tip the nectarines and almonds into a large roasting tin. Scatter over the rosemary, drizzle over the honey, then cover with the torn focaccia. Drizzle the olive oil over the focaccia, then transfer to the oven and roast for 25–30 minutes, until the bread is toasted and the nectarines are cooked through.

Meanwhile, whisk the extra virgin olive oil, honey and balsamic together for the dressing.

If serving in the tin, gently stir the watercress and dressing through the salad and top with the goat's cheese before serving.

If you're making a plated starter, divide the watercress between 4 plates, then arrange the nectarines and focaccia over them. Add the goat's cheese and the almonds, then drizzle the dressing over before serving warm.

BAKED FETA CHEESE WITH FIGS, PINE NUTS & BASIL

This dish is so lovely that I would have it for breakfast. Feta cheese works so well with the figs and honey that it's perfect as a light dinner party starter, or as part of a more informal sharing table. If you use a shallower tin, the cheese will crisp and turn golden brown, while the deeper tin we used for the photo opposite will give you a softer finish.

Serves: 4 as a starter, or as
         part of a spread
Prep: 10 minutes
Cook: 20–25 minutes

2 x 200g blocks of feta cheese
8 figs, halved
1 tablespoon olive oil
2 tablespoons honey
Freshly ground black pepper
50g pine nuts
1/2 lemon, zest and juice
   (use 1 lemon if your lemon
   isn't very juicy)
1 tablespoon extra virgin olive oil
20g fresh basil, leaves finely
   sliced
Good crusty bread or sourdough,
   to serve

Preheat the oven to 180°C fan/200°C/gas 6. Cut each block of feta in half, then pop the pieces into a roasting tin with the figs surrounding them. Drizzle everything with the olive oil and honey, add a good grind of pepper, throw over the pine nuts, then transfer to the oven and roast for 20–25 minutes, until the figs have softened.

Just before the traybake is ready, mix the lemon zest, juice, extra virgin olive oil and basil. Pour it over the figs and feta as soon as they come out of the oven, then serve hot with good crusty bread on the side.

ROSEMARY & GARLIC ROASTED LAMB WITH ARTICHOKES & OLIVES

This stunning traybake delivers on all fronts: the artichokes, olives and lamb work beautifully together, while the cannellini beans soak up all the wonderful flavours from the tin at the end. Perfect for easy entertaining. If you're prepping in advance, just stick everything in the tin, pop it into the fridge and take it out 15 minutes before you're ready to cook, bearing in mind that if it's all super cold, it'll take a little longer in the oven.

Serves: 4
Prep: 10 minutes
Cook: 20-25 minutes

350g cherry tomatoes on the vine
1 x 290g jar of artichokes, drained, plus 1 tablespoon oil from the jar
165g pitted black olives
8 free-range lamb loin chops (allow 150-200g lamb per person)
2-3 sprigs of fresh rosemary leaves, finely chopped
2 cloves of garlic, crushed
1 teaspoon sea salt flakes
1 x 400g tin of cannellini beans, drained and rinsed
1 lemon, juice only
A handful of fresh basil or flat-leaf parsley, chopped

Preheat the oven to 180°C fan/200°C/gas 6. Tip the cherry tomatoes with their vines, the artichokes and olives into a roasting tin. Rub the lamb chops with the artichoke oil, then scatter them with the rosemary, crushed garlic and a pinch of salt before nestling them in the tin along with the artichokes and olives.

Transfer to the oven and bake for 20 minutes for lamb that is blushing pink. If your steaks are quite thick, leave them in for a little longer, just under 25 minutes.

Stir the cannellini beans and lemon juice through the tomatoes and olives. Leave the steaks to rest for 5 minutes before scattering over the basil or parsley and serving hot.

CHANGE IT UP: Think your guests won't like lamb? Follow the recipe above but with chicken breasts, leaving them in the oven for 25-30 minutes, until cooked through.

SESAME & THYME ROASTED CAULIFLOWER PILAF WITH FETA CHEESE & WATERCRESS

Za'atar is one of my favourite spice mixes. It's usually made with toasted sesame seeds, salt, sumac, dried thyme, marjoram or oregano. It's readily available in big supermarkets, but if you can't find any for this recipe, use a tablespoon each of dried thyme and sesame seeds. This pilaf makes a lovely side dish when entertaining, but paired with the charred broccoli on page 152 or the masala corn on page 156, it works perfectly as part of a vegetarian sharing feast.

Serves: 4 as a side
Prep: 10 minutes
Cook: 20–25 minutes

200g bulgur wheat, rinsed
400ml hot vegetable stock
1 red onion, roughly sliced
$2^1/_2$ cm fresh ginger, grated
Leaves from the cauliflower,
 roughly chopped
1 large cauliflower, cut into
 small florets
1 tablespoon olive oil
2 heaped tablespoons za'atar
2 cloves of garlic, crushed
1 lemon, zest and juice
1 tablespoon extra virgin olive oil
1 bag of watercress (85–100g),
 roughly chopped
100g feta cheese
5 radishes, finely sliced

Preheat the oven to 200°C fan/220°C/gas 7. Tip the bulgur wheat, stock, onion, ginger and cauliflower leaves into a roasting tin and stir, making sure the bulgur is covered with the liquid. On your chopping board, rub the cauliflower with the oil, za'atar and crushed garlic, then scatter it over the bulgur wheat.

Transfer the tin to the oven and bake for 20–25 minutes, until the cauliflower is charred and just cooked through. Remove from the oven and stir through the lemon juice, extra virgin olive oil and watercress. Top with the feta cheese and radishes and serve hot.

CHANGE IT UP: You can easily veganise this dish by leaving out the feta cheese and adding a good handful of toasted almonds. (If you aren't vegan, you can still add extra almonds.)

SICHUAN PEPPERED PORK CHOPS WITH APPLES & CABBAGE

Sichuan peppercorns are possibly my favourite kitchen ingredient and I use them in almost everything. This is the only time in the book where I'd encourage you to buy a bag of peppercorns from a Chinese grocery shop or online, as they're so much more aromatic than those you can get at the supermarket.

Serves: 4
Prep: 10 minutes
Cook: 30 minutes

1 large sweetheart cabbage, quartered, then cut into ¹/₂ cm slices
4 apples, each cut into 8
4 teaspoons Sichuan peppercorns
2 teaspoons sea salt flakes
2 tablespoons sesame oil
20g unsalted butter, sliced
4 x 200g free-range pork chops (about 1¹/₂ cm thick)
2 cloves of garlic, crushed
1 lemon, juice only
Hot basmati rice, to serve

Preheat the oven to 200°C fan/220°C/gas 7. Mix the sweetheart cabbage, apples and 1 teaspoon of Sichuan peppercorns, 1 teaspoon of sea salt and 1 tablespoon of sesame oil in a roasting tin, and dot with the sliced butter. Transfer to the oven and roast for 10 minutes.

Meanwhile, get your pork chops and rub them with the rest of the Sichuan peppercorns, the crushed garlic, another teaspoon of sea salt flakes and another tablespoon of sesame oil.

Once the cabbage has had 10 minutes, reduce the oven temperature to 180°C fan/200°C/ gas 6, remove the tin from the oven, lay the pork chops over the top and return it to the oven for a further 20 minutes, until the chops are just cooked through.

Squeeze the lemon juice over the pork and veg and taste a bit of cabbage to assess if you need a pinch more sea salt. Let it rest for 5 minutes, then serve the chops hot, with the apples and cabbage alongside. This is lovely with buttery white rice.

NOTES: You can use ordinary white cabbage if you can't find sweetheart. If you're using salted butter, don't add salt with the apples at step 1.

ROASTED HALLOUMI WITH AUBERGINES, TOMATOES & PINE NUTS

This is a wonderful celebratory dish and I love the mix of colours and textures: golden baked halloumi, crisp pine nuts, soft aubergines and a little kick from the chilli flakes. Fresh oregano, if you can get it, adds an incredible flavour to the aubergines; it's quite unlike dried, so use fresh rosemary as an alternative if you need to.

Serves: 4
Prep: 10 minutes
Cook: 30 minutes

400g cherry tomatoes
  on the vine, halved
2 medium aubergines,
  cut into 1cm half moons
400–500g halloumi,
  cut into 1cm slices
7–8 sprigs of fresh oregano,
  leaves only
2 tablespoons olive oil
1 teaspoon chilli flakes
2 cloves of garlic, crushed
40g pine nuts
100g rocket, roughly chopped
1 lemon, juice only

Preheat the oven to 200°C fan/220°C/gas 7. Tip everything except the pine nuts, rocket and lemon juice into a roasting tin and mix well with your hands. Use a tin large enough to have the aubergines all in a single layer. Now arrange the ingredients so the halloumi sits on top.

Transfer to the oven and roast for 20 minutes, then scatter the pine nuts on top before roasting for a further 10 minutes until the halloumi is golden brown and the aubergines are cooked through.

Stir through the rocket and lemon juice and serve hot.

SERVE WITH: This is lovely with a pile of warm flatbreads and some yogurt.

TANDOORI-STYLE SALMON WITH SPICED, ROASTED SWEET POTATOES, TOMATOES & RED ONION

This is my all-in-one dinner version of my sister Padmini's tandoori salmon, one of our favourite weeknight dinners when we were flatmates. It works beautifully with the lightly spiced sweet potato and tomatoes, just make sure you use one or two tins big enough to get all the sweet potatoes in a single layer, and cut the sweet potatoes into very small pieces so they cook in 30 minutes. .

Serves: 4
Prep: 10 minutes
Cook: 30 minutes

3 cloves of garlic, grated
4cm fresh ginger, grated
75g natural yogurt
1 lemon, zest only
2 scant teaspoons ground cumin
1 scant teaspoon ground turmeric
1 teaspoon smoked paprika
½ teaspoon mild chilli powder
A large pinch of sea salt flakes
4 salmon fillets
Natural yogurt, to serve

FOR THE SWEET POTATOES
650g sweet potatoes, peeled
  and cut into 1cm cubes
2 tablespoons vegetable oil
1 teaspoon ground cumin
1 teaspoon sea salt flakes
400g cherry tomatoes on
  the vine
1 red onion, roughly sliced

Mix the garlic, ginger, yogurt, lemon zest, spices and salt together and gently turn the salmon fillets over in this mixture. (This can be marinated in the fridge if you are preparing this ahead.)

When ready to cook, preheat the oven to 210°C fan/230°C/gas 8. Tip the cubed sweet potatoes into a roasting tin large enough to hold everything in a single layer, mix them with the oil, cumin and salt, then transfer to the oven and roast for 10 minutes.

Once the sweet potatoes have had 10 minutes, tip the cherry tomatoes, their vines and the sliced onion into the tin, and mix well. Use a wooden spoon to make 4 spaces for the salmon fillets and gently pop them into the tin. Reduce the oven temperature to 180°C fan/200°C/gas 6, then return the tin to the oven for a final 20 minutes.

Serve the salmon and vegetables with the natural yogurt alongside.

MAKE IT VEGGIE: Leave out the fish. Tear up large chunks of shop-bought paneer into roughly 5cm pieces, marinating them as above, and stir through some lime-dressed chopped spinach at the end.

SPICED LAMB MEATBALLS WITH SUMAC ROASTED CAULIFLOWER & POMEGRANATE

Think about the best lamb kofte or kebabs you've ever had and you'll have an idea of how flavoursome this dish is. The warming spices in the lamb work perfectly with the pomegranates and lemony cauliflower. Serve with flatbreads or cous cous.

Serves: 4
Prep: 10 minutes
Cook: 25 minutes

FOR THE MEATBALLS

400g minced, free-range lamb
1 small onion, roughly chopped
1 teaspoon mild chilli powder
1 teaspoon ground coriander
1 teaspoon ground cumin
1 teaspoon sea salt flakes
1 free-range egg
2 heaped teaspoons gram
   (chickpea) flour (optional)
15g fresh mint leaves

FOR THE REST

1 large cauliflower, cut into
   medium-sized florets plus
   the leaves
3 heaped teaspoons sumac
2 teaspoons ground cumin
1 teaspoon sea salt flakes
1 tablespoon olive oil
1 lemon, zest and juice
1 tablespoon extra virgin olive oil
1 pomegranate, seeds only
A handful flat-leaf parsley
   leaves, chopped
1 tablespoon pomegranate
   molasses (optional)

Preheat the oven to 180°C fan/200°C/gas 6. Tip all the meatball ingredients into a food processor and blitz briefly until everything comes together evenly.

Tip the cauliflower, leaves, spices, salt and oil into a large roasting tin and mix until everything is evenly spiced.

With damp hands (I keep a bowl of water nearby), take walnut-sized pieces of the lamb mix and roll them into small meatballs. Dot them among the cauliflower pieces as you go – you should have about 20–22.

Transfer to the oven and roast for 25 minutes, until the tops of the meatballs are evenly coloured and the cauliflower is cooked through. Whisk the lemon zest, juice and extra virgin olive oil together, drizzle this over the traybake, then scatter over the pomegranate seeds and parsley. Drizzle over the pomegranate molasses (if using) and serve the traybake hot.

NOTE: If you already have some gram or chickpea flour in the cupboard, it adds a really silky texture to the finished meatballs, but don't worry if you don't have any in, as they're still gorgeous.

CHARRED TENDERSTEM WITH BLACK BEANS, AVOCADO & PEANUTS

This might be one of my favourite dishes in the book. The combination of crisp, roasted black beans and broccoli with creamy avocado and lime juice is just stunning. Consider having a tray of this to yourself for dinner, then you won't have to share it with anyone. . . though if you're making a vegetarian or vegan grazing feast, it goes very well with the masala roasted corn on page 156.

Serves: 4 as a side
Prep: 10 minutes
Cook: 20 minutes

400g Tenderstem broccoli
1 x 400g tin of black beans,
   drained and rinsed
1 red onion, roughly sliced
2 cloves of garlic, crushed
1 scant teaspoon chipotle
   chilli flakes
1 tablespoon olive oil
1 teaspoon sea salt
2 limes, zest and juice
1 tablespoon extra virgin olive oil
2 avocados, peeled and sliced
A large handful of salted peanuts,
   finely chopped

Preheat the oven to 200°C fan/220°C/gas 7. Put the Tenderstem into a bowl and pour over a kettleful of boiling water. Let it sit for a minute, then drain it really well, pat it dry with a tea towel and tip it into a roasting tin. (This blanching stage might seem like a minor faff, but it massively improves the texture of the broccoli when it's roasted.)

Tip in the black beans and red onion, then mix through the crushed garlic, chilli flakes and olive oil, making sure to work plenty of oil into the ends of the broccoli, as that'll help it to crisp up. Scatter over the sea salt, then transfer to the oven and roast for 15–20 minutes, until the broccoli is nicely charred.

Meanwhile, whisk the lime zest, juice and extra virgin olive oil together.

Once the broccoli is cooked, stir through the dressing along with the sliced avocados and chopped peanuts. Taste and adjust the lime juice if needed (there should be enough salt from the peanuts). Serve immediately.

CHANGE IT UP: For a weeknight meal for two, stir through roughly chopped lamb's lettuce or watercress and serve with brown rice.

MASALA ROASTED CORN WITH QUICK CORIANDER CHUTNEY

I love corn on the cob, but to max the flavour on this – and make it slightly easier for you and your guests to eat – it works really well if you slice the kernels off the cob post-cooking. That way they pick up all the flavour from the roasting tin and the chutney. Using those little half-sized corn on the cob makes them easier to slice, though four ordinary sized cobs would work well too. A lovely colourful dish.

Serves: 4
Prep: 10 minutes
Cook: 30 minutes

8 half-sized corn on the cob, or 4 full-sized
2 red onions, quartered
1 x 400g tin of chickpeas, drained and rinsed
4 cloves of garlic, crushed
2 tablespoons olive oil
2 teaspoons ground cumin
2 teaspoons ground coriander
2 teaspoons smoked paprika
1 teaspoon mild chilli powder
2 teaspoons sea salt flakes

FOR THE CHUTNEY
50g coriander, finely chopped
100g coconut or natural yogurt
1 lemon, juice only
1 teaspoon sea salt flakes

Preheat the oven to 180°C fan/200°C/gas 6. Tip the corn, onions and chickpeas into a roasting tin and mix well with the garlic, oil, spices and salt. Transfer to the oven and roast for 30 minutes.

Meanwhile, stir the coriander, yogurt, lemon juice and sea salt together for the chutney. It'll be a really thick paste, so let it down by stirring in 1 tablespoon of water at a time, until you have a thick but pourable consistency. Taste and adjust the lemon and salt as needed.

Once the corn is cooked, give it a moment to cool down, then take each cob and stand it upright on a chopping board. Slice the kernels off, then return them to the tin and stir through the rest of the roasted ingredients. Serve with the chutney alongside.

NOTE: You won't get the same texture from roasting a drained tin of sweetcorn, which is why it's best to roast the cobs whole, then get the kernels off.

SPICED ROAST CHICKEN WITH PEPPERS, AUBERGINE & ONION

An easy, all-in-one chicken traybake for a casual dinner with friends, packed with flavourful vegetables. Rather than a long list of spices, I like to use ras-el-hanout for this. It's a readily available Middle Eastern spice mix that adds a lovely warming flavour to the dish. It isn't hot in the way that chilli is, so if your guests like spicy food, add a teaspoon of chilli flakes as well.

Serves: 4
Prep: 10 minutes
Cook: 25–30 minutes

1 large aubergine,
    cut into 1½ cm cubes
2 red peppers, cut into 1cm slices
1 yellow pepper, cut into 1cm
    slices
1 red onion, roughly sliced
4 vine tomatoes, quartered
3 cloves of garlic
4 heaped teaspoons
    ras-el- hanout
2 tablespoons olive oil
1 teaspoon sea salt flakes
4 free-range chicken breasts
    (halved if very large)

TO SERVE
A handful of fresh coriander,
    chopped
Natural yogurt
Cous cous or flatbreads

Preheat the oven to 180°C fan/200°C/gas 6. Tip the aubergine, peppers, onion, tomatoes and garlic into a large roasting tin along with 2 teaspoons of the ras-el-hanout, 1 tablespoon of olive oil and the sea salt flakes. Mix really well with your hands.

Arrange the chicken breasts over the vegetables and drizzle the other tablespoon of oil over them, followed by a good pinch of salt and the remaining ras-el-hanout. Transfer to the oven and roast for 25–30 minutes, until the chicken is cooked through.

Serve scattered with the fresh coriander, with yogurt on the side along with a pile of flatbreads or buttery cous cous.

ROAST SWEET POTATO WITH OREGANO, FETA CHEESE & CHARRED LEMON

Confession – I forgot to put the lemons into the dish opposite before we took the photograph, because I'd forgotten to write them into the ingredient list – now amended. It happens. You should definitely try to remember to put them in, though, as the baked lemon gives a really lovely flavour to the potatoes and feta cheese, plus you can squash them down and they form a sort of instant, sharp dressing.

Serves: 4–6 as a side
Prep: 10 minutes
Cook: 30 minutes

750g sweet potato, peeled
 and cut into $1/2$ cm half moons
$2^1/2$ tablespoons olive oil
$1/2$ teaspoon sea salt
1 bulb of garlic, skin on, halved
1 lemon, cut into wedges
400g feta cheese, roughly broken
 into large pieces
8–9 sprigs of fresh oregano,
 leaves only
2–3 sprigs of fresh rosemary
Freshly ground black pepper
Natural yogurt, to serve

Preheat the oven to 200°C fan/220°C/gas 7. Mix the sweet potatoes, 2 tablespoons of the olive oil and the sea salt in a roasting tin large enough to hold everything in a single layer. (Use 2 tins if your largest one is too small.)

Put the halved garlic and lemon wedges into the tin and scatter over the feta pieces, followed by the herbs. Drizzle the cheese and garlic with the remaining oil, give everything a good grind of black pepper, then transfer to the oven and roast for 30 minutes.

Serve hot, squeezing out the roasted lemons to 'dress' the dish. This is nice with a spoonful of cold yogurt.

WEEKEND COOKING

EASY TRAYBAKES TO STICK ON
FOR A LATE MORNING BRUNCH
OR WEEKEND LUNCH

WEEKEND COOKING

BREAKFAST TART WITH PANCETTA,
EGGS & ASPARAGUS

BREAKFAST PANCAKE WITH BERRIES & LEMON BUTTER (V)

BAKED EGGS WITH ASPARAGUS SOLDIERS (V)

WEEKEND BREAKFAST TRAYBAKE

CRISP CHEDDAR-TOPPED BREAD COBBLER
WITH CHILLI SPIKED GREENS (V)

SCANDI-STYLE MEATBALLS WITH FENNEL,
BEETROOT & DILL

ONE POT PEANUT CHILLI CHICKEN
WITH TOMATO RICE

BEETROOT & LEEK GRATIN WITH GOAT'S CHEESE
& HAZELNUTS (V)

SAFFRON FISH STEW WITH FENNEL & LEEKS

PORK, JUNIPER & PINK PEPPERCORN MEATBALLS
WITH LEEKS & PUY LENTILS

BREAKFAST TART WITH PANCETTA, EGGS & ASPARAGUS

Obviously, I couldn't have a chapter in this book without a puff pastry tart or three. This variation is inspired by an absolutely stunning dish in my pal Richard Burr's cookbook *BIY*, which I still remember wolfing down in about three minutes. Try either if you've got friends staying over at the weekend. The spring onions help cut the richness of the bacon and eggs.

Serves: 4
Prep: 10 minutes
Cook: 25–30 minutes

1 x 320g ready-rolled
   puff pastry sheet
2 teaspoons Dijon mustard
95g thinly sliced pancetta
   or streaky bacon
200g asparagus spears
5 spring onions, finely sliced
4 free-range eggs
Freshly ground black pepper

Preheat the oven to 180°C fan/200°C/gas 6. Lay out the puff pastry on a baking sheet, leaving it on the paper that it came in, and spread it with the mustard, leaving a 1 $\frac{1}{2}$ cm border around the edges.

Lay the pancetta or bacon over the tart from side to side, leaving about a 2 $\frac{1}{2}$ cm gap between the slices, then lay the asparagus over them. Scatter the spring onions around the edges of the veg and bacon as it'll help prevent the eggs going everywhere later. Transfer the tart to the oven and bake for 15 minutes.

After 15 minutes, remove the tray from the oven and crack the eggs over the tart. Season them well with freshly ground black pepper, then return to the oven and bake for a further 10–15 minutes, until the eggs are cooked to your liking. Serve hot.

NOTE: The fresher the eggs you use here, the more likely they are to behave when you crack them over the tart: the whites will stay together in a neat egg shape.

BREAKFAST PANCAKE WITH BERRIES & LEMON BUTTER

I'm not sure there's anything better than pancakes for a weekend breakfast, unless it's pancakes that don't require standing and flipping at the stove. This recipe, inspired by my favourite Curtis Stone ricotta pancakes, will make the most beautifully light, fluffy oven pancake, with a crisp top and edges. If you haven't got ricotta in the house, a tub of cottage cheese from the corner shop works perfectly as a replacement.

Serves: 4
Prep: 10 minutes
Cook: 25–30 minutes

50g unsalted butter
250g ricotta or cottage cheese
4 free-range eggs
200ml milk
50g caster sugar
150g plain flour
1$\frac{1}{2}$ teaspoons baking powder
Big handfuls of raspberries,
   blueberries & blackberries
   (frozen is fine here)
Icing sugar, to dust

TO SERVE
100g softened unsalted butter
30g icing sugar
1 tablespoon lemon juice
$\frac{1}{2}$ a lemon, zest and juice

Preheat the oven to 200°C fan/220°C/gas 7. Put the butter into the roasting tin and pop the tin into the oven for the butter to melt.

Beat the ricotta or cottage cheese, eggs, milk and sugar together, then pour in the melted butter from the tin. Stir through the flour and baking powder until smooth, then pour the batter into the hot buttery roasting tin.

Scatter over the berries, then return to the oven to bake for 25–30 minutes, until golden brown and well risen.

Meanwhile, beat the softened butter, icing sugar, lemon zest and juice together.

Dust the pancake with the icing sugar, then cut into slices and serve hot with the lemon butter alongside.

BAKED EGGS WITH ASPARAGUS SOLDIERS

These eggs, baked in a blanket of crème fraîche with a mushroom and spring onion, are inspired by Rachel Khoo and a quick fridge forage for ingredients. Serve with mountains of hot buttered toast (cut into soldiers, of course). I give the quantities per person, because then it's easy to scale up if you're serving two, four, or having a luxurious breakfast for one.

Serves: 1
Prep: 5 minutes
Cook: 15 minutes

2 heaped tablespoons
  crème fraîche
1 medium-sized mushroom,
  finely chopped
1/2 spring onion, finely chopped
Sea salt flakes and freshly ground
  black pepper
1 free-range egg
5–6 asparagus spears
A tiny bit of olive oil
Freshly made buttered
  toast soldiers

Preheat the oven to 180°C fan/200°C/gas 6. You will need a small ramekin per egg. Put 1 heaped tablespoon of crème fraîche at the bottom of your ramekin, then top with the finely chopped mushroom, half the spring onion and a good pinch of salt and freshly ground black pepper.

Crack the egg in over the mushrooms, then gently top with another heaped tablespoon of crème fraîche and the remaining spring onion. Season with salt and pepper, then put the ramekin into a roasting tin.

Pop the asparagus spears in the tin alongside, dress them with the olive oil, salt and pepper, then transfer to the oven and bake for 12–15 minutes, until the egg is just set, but still dippable. (Cook for longer if you prefer your egg more set.)

Serve the egg and asparagus with buttered toast soldiers.

NOTE: This is one of the few recipes where having a slightly differently temperatured oven will make a difference to the finished dish. I'd recommend watching the egg from 10 minutes, giving it a prod, then returning to the oven if needed.

WEEKEND BREAKFAST TRAYBAKE

My weekend breakfasts (when not based around pancakes) almost always involve mushrooms, spinach, tomatoes and eggs. Ususally I'd roast the tomatoes, fry the mushrooms, wilt the spinach and fry the eggs, leaving four pans, a tin and a colander to wash up as well as the coffee pot. I'm not sure why it took me so long to realise you can do it all in one tin . . .

Serves: 2–4 (depending how many eggs you want per person)
Prep: 10 minutes
Cook: 30 minutes

300g portobello mushrooms, halved
1 red onion, roughly chopped
300g cherry tomatoes on the vine
200g cooking chorizo, cut into 1½ cm chunks (alternatively, use mini cooking chorizo)
1 tablespoon olive oil
160g spinach, roughly chopped
4 free-range eggs
Hot buttered toast, to serve

Preheat the oven to 200°C fan/220°C/gas 7. Mix the mushrooms, red onion, cherry tomatoes with their vines, the cooking chorizo and the oil in a roasting tin large enough to hold everything in a single layer, then transfer to the oven and roast for 15 minutes.

After 15 minutes, reduce the oven temperature to 160°C fan/180°C/gas 4 and stir through the chopped spinach. Make 2 to 4 wells in the traybake, crack the eggs in, then return to the oven to cook for a further 7–12 minutes, until to your liking.

Serve with plenty of hot buttered toast.

CRISP CHEDDAR-TOPPED BREAD COBBLER WITH CHILLI SPIKED GREENS

This is easily one of my favourite creations, born out of thinking of a savoury bread and butter pudding, cheese on toast, and how nice cabbage can be when it's buttery, hot and ideally served with cream. Livened up with chilli, garlic and sage, this all-in-one meal is perfect for a cold evening and, if you're anything like me, you'll be living off it from autumn onwards.

Serves: 4 generously
Prep: 15 minutes
Cook: 25 minutes

1 sweetheart cabbage, halved, cored and cut into $1/2$ cm slices
1 small head of broccoli, cut into small florets
1 small onion, roughly chopped
2 cloves of garlic, crushed
1 teaspoon chilli flakes
14 fresh sage leaves, half roughly chopped, the rest left whole
250ml vegetable stock (use 1 stock cube and 250ml water)
500g crème fraîche
2 heaped teaspoons Dijon mustard
2 free-range eggs
60g cheddar cheese, grated
1 heaped teaspoon sea salt flakes
250g good stale bread, cut into 1cm slices and buttered

Preheat the oven to 200°C fan/220°C/gas 7. Mix the cabbage, broccoli, onion, garlic, chilli flakes and chopped sage leaves in a medium-sized deep roasting tin or lasagne dish, then pour over the stock.

Whisk the crème fraîche, mustard, eggs, half the grated cheese and the salt together, then spread half of this over the veg.

Thickly pave the tin with the sliced bread (I like to halve mine to look like cobblestones, see opposite), then pour the remaining crème fraîche and mustard mixture evenly over this. Use a big spoon to smooth and squash this so the bread is well covered. Scatter it with the remaining whole sage leaves and some grated cheddar cheese.

Transfer to the oven and bake for 25 minutes, until the top is golden brown and crisp, then serve hot. This is great heated through in the oven the next day too, if you have leftovers.

NOTE: If your bread isn't very stale to start with, consider putting the slices into the preheating oven to dry out while you prepare the vegetables (if the bread is too fresh, it won't get as crisp).

SCANDI-STYLE MEATBALLS
WITH FENNEL, BEETROOT & DILL

This dish was born out of a shopping trip with my friend Danielle, where we ate meatballs, insane quantities of lingonberry jam, mashed potatoes (me) and chips (her) before attempting to navigate the three-floored heaven/hell that is the North London IKEA. She very kindly brainstormed this dish with me on the bus home, transforming it from a slightly odd traybake involving rhubarb into the rather lovely recipe below.

Serves: 4
Prep: 10 minutes
Cook: 25 minutes

2 fennel bulbs, very finely sliced
3 medium beetroot, grated
1 x 400g tin of cannellini beans,
   drained and rinsed
2 cloves of garlic, minced
1 tablespoon olive oil
200ml chicken stock, made with
   1 stock cube or little plastic tub,
   plus 300ml water
500g minced free-range pork
1 heaped teaspoon Dijon mustard
20g fresh dill, chopped, plus a
   handful to serve
$\frac{1}{2}$ teaspoon fennel seeds
1 free-range egg
100ml soured cream, to serve

Preheat the oven to 180°C fan/200°C/gas 6. Mix the fennel, beetroot, beans, garlic, oil and stock in a roasting tin large enough to hold the veg comfortably without over-crowding.

Blitz the minced pork, mustard, dill, fennel seeds and egg together, then form into 24 walnut-sized meatballs. Dot these over the beetroot mix, then transfer to the oven and roast for 25 minutes, until the meatballs are cooked through.

Stir the soured cream through the stew and scatter over the dill before serving.

NOTE: It's quite useful to get a helper on this, so one of you can grate the beetroot and the other can make the meatballs. If you have a food processor with a grating attachment, definitely use that. Feta cheese is a non-Scandi addition, but if you have leftover meatballs the next day, I highly recommend scattering it all over them before re-baking at 180°C fan/200°C/gas 6 for 20 minutes.

ONE POT PEANUT CHILLI CHICKEN WITH TOMATO RICE

This is the ultimate Saturday night, bowl in front of the television food and can be made even when you think your energy reserves could not be lower. Peanut, chilli and chicken is one of my favourite flavour combinations, whether in a groundnut stew (see the recipe in Ruby Tandoh's *Flavour*) or here, spiked with soy and sesame oil. The rice helpfully cooks along with the chicken, so you need do nothing more than decide what to watch.

Serves: 4
Prep: 10 minutes
Cook: 30 minutes

200g basmati rice
300g cherry tomatoes on
   the vine
400ml boiling chicken stock
60g crunchy peanut butter
1 red chilli, finely chopped
1 tablespoon sesame oil
1 tablespoon dark soy sauce
1 lime, juice only
8 free-range, boneless, skinless
   chicken thighs

FOR THE DRESSING
$\frac{1}{2}$ tablespoon dark soy sauce
1 tablespoon lime juice
1 tablespoon sesame oil

TO SERVE
A handful of peanuts
3 spring onions, finely sliced
25g fresh coriander, chopped

Preheat the oven to 210°C fan/230°C/gas 8. Tip the rice into a lidded casserole dish or medium deep roasting tin, along with the tomatoes and their vines. Then pour over the boiling chicken stock.

Mix the peanut butter, red chilli, sesame oil, soy sauce and lime juice together. Lay the chicken thighs over the rice and tomatoes, pour the peanut butter mixture over and smooth it down, then cover with the lid or very tightly with foil (this is really important, as the rice needs a very tight seal to cook properly). Transfer to the oven and bake for 30 minutes.

Once the chicken is cooked and the peanut butter has formed a lovely golden crust, mix the soy, lime juice and sesame oil for the dressing. Pour it over the chicken and rice, scatter over the peanuts, spring onions and coriander and serve hot.

NOTE: Don't try to use chicken thighs on the bone as they won't cook in half an hour.

BEETROOT & LEEK GRATIN WITH GOAT'S CHEESE & HAZELNUTS

I love a gratin: the way it bubbles out of the dish, the crisp topping burning your mouth on the first bite. By using grated fresh beetroot instead of sliced, this ruby beauty with leeks and fennel is easily ready in half an hour, and works beautifully with the hazelnuts and goat's cheese. It's rich and comforting.

Serves: 4
Prep: 10 minutes
Cook: 30 minutes

2 large leeks, finely sliced
2 bulbs of fennel, finely sliced
300g raw beetroot, grated
  (about 4)
2–3 sprigs of fresh rosemary,
  leaves roughly chopped
500g crème fraîche
1 teaspoon sea salt
Freshly ground black pepper
200g goat's cheese, sliced or
  crumbled
40g panko breadcrumbs
50g hazelnuts, roughly chopped
1 tablespoon olive oil
$1/2$ a lemon, juice only

Preheat the oven to 200°C fan/220°C/gas 7. Pop the sliced leeks and fennel into a large bowl and pour over a kettleful of boiling water. Leave to sit for 2 minutes, then drain and tip into a large roasting tin. Stir through the beetroot, rosemary, crème fraîche and salt.

Scatter over some freshly ground black pepper, then top with the goat's cheese, breadcrumbs and hazelnuts. Drizzle with the olive oil, then transfer to the oven and bake for 30 minutes.

The gratin will look alarmingly soupy when you take it out of the oven, but don't panic. Leave it to sit for 10 minutes and it'll settle down, then serve hot, with a good squeeze of lemon juice.

NOTE: This gratin is fabulous made in advance and reheated, so it's a good recipe to make on the weekend for an easy side during the week.

SAFFRON FISH STEW WITH FENNEL & LEEKS

Otherwise known as bouillabaisse, the classic Provençal fish stew. For a definitive description of the dish, see John Lanchester's *A Debt to Pleasure*. This version uses many of his suggested ingredients, but in an easy, quick oven version, perfect for a relaxed weekend lunch. Serve with lots of crusty bread to mop up the soup.

Serves: 4
Prep: 10 minutes
Cook: 30 minutes

220g cherry tomatoes on the vine, halved
1 bulb of fennel, halved and very finely sliced
2 cloves of garlic, crushed
1 small leek, halved and finely sliced
2 strips of orange zest
1 bay leaf
A good pinch of saffron threads
500ml good fish stock
50ml olive oil
500g mixed fish fillets (think salmon, smoked haddock, cod, large raw prawns or monkfish if you are feeling fancy; fish can be ready-cubed as fish pie mix)
Sea salt flakes, to taste
1 lemon, juice only
Frondy fennel tops or a few sprigs of fresh dill, to serve (optional)
Crusty bread and butter, to serve

Preheat the oven to 180°C fan/200°C/gas 6. Tip everything except the fish, salt, lemon juice, and fennel tops or dill into a small deep roasting tin or lidded casserole dish. Don't forget to include the tomato vines – as ever, they're your secret ingredient for maximising flavour. Cover the dish with tightly scrunched foil or a lid, then transfer to the oven and bake for 20 minutes.

If you haven't bought ready-cubed fish pie mix, cut your fish fillets into 2 $\frac{1}{2}$ cm pieces.

Once the broth has had 20 minutes, remove the tin or casserole dish from the oven, then use a wooden spoon to squash the tomatoes down. Add the mixed fish, then return the dish to the oven uncovered and cook for a further 7 or so minutes, until just cooked through. (The broth is so hot that the fish and prawns will cook very quickly.)

Fish out the tomato vines, taste and adjust the seasoning with salt and lemon juice as needed, scatter over the fennel tops or dill (if using) and serve immediately, with crusty bread and butter.

PORK, JUNIPER & PINK PEPPERCORN MEATBALLS WITH LEEKS & PUY LENTILS

These are some of the nicest meatballs I've ever had and it's well worth looking at the spice section in the supermarket for the slightly more unusual juniper berries and pink peppercorns (they won't go to waste, as you'll definitely want to make these again). Use good-quality sausages, as the texture works really well here and you'll need the added seasoning from them.

Serves: 2–3
Prep: 10 minutes
Cook: 25–30 minutes

3 leeks, halved and cut into
   1cm half-moons
1 x 250g vac pack of cooked
   Puy lentils
1 tablespoon olive oil
1 teaspoon sea salt flakes
1 tablespoon juniper berries
1 tablespoon pink peppercorns
1 lemon, zest and juice
1 free-range egg, beaten
6 free-range pork sausages
1 tablespoon extra virgin olive oil
A handful of fresh flat-leaf
   parsley leaves, finely chopped

Preheat the oven to 180°C fan/200°C/gas 6. Tip the leeks and Puy lentils into a roasting tin with the olive oil and sea salt and mix well.

Grind the juniper and pink peppercorns to a rough powder, then add them to a bowl with the lemon zest and egg.

Squeeze the sausagemeat from the sausage casings into the bowl and mix well with your hands until everything is evenly incorporated. Take walnut-sized balls of the mixture (this is easier with wet hands) and form into meatballs, popping them into the roasting tin as you go. You should have about 18 meatballs by the end.

Transfer the tin to the oven and bake for 25–30 minutes, until the meatballs are golden and crisp on top.

Whisk the lemon juice, extra virgin olive oil and a pinch of sea salt together and dress the meatballs and lentils with it. Scatter with the parsley and a pinch more of the pink peppercorns if you like and serve hot.

SWEETS

ONE TIN TREATS FROM WEEKEND
BAKING TO DINNER PARTY
DESSERTS. ALL VEGETARIAN,
SOME VEGAN

SWEETS

CHOCOLATE, SAGE & SEA SALT GIANT COOKIE (V)

BLACKBERRY & PISTACHIO CAKE (V)

POMEGRANATE YOGURT CAKE (V)

SALTED CHOCOLATE PEANUT BROWNIES (V)

ROASTED APRICOTS WITH A ROSEMARY
& HAZELNUT CRUMBLE (V)

CINNAMON CHERRY CLAFOUTIS (V)

PECAN CHOCOLATE CHIP BANANA BREAD (VEGAN)

GINGERBREAD PEARS (V)

APPLE CRUMBLE CAKE (V)

CARAMELISED BANANA & THYME TARTE TATIN (VEGAN)

COFFEE & BAILEYS CAKE (V)

CHOCOLATE, SAGE & SEA SALT GIANT COOKIE

This is the chocolate chip cookie of dreams, the kind that will make your home smell – in the best possible way – like a shopping mall cookie-vending concession. In honour of those, it's a giant traybake cookie, but with a distinctly grown-up edge from the sage and sea salt. Use the darkest, best quality chocolate chips you can find and a generous hand with the sea salt.

Serves: depends how much cookie you eat –
6 hungry, 8 moderate,
10 abstemious
Prep: 10 minutes
Cook: 20–25 minutes

225g soft light brown sugar
250g softened unsalted butter,
  plus more for the tin
10 fresh sage leaves, finely
  chopped, plus 4–5 left whole
2 medium free-range eggs
350g plain flour
$^1\!/_2$ teaspoon baking powder
1 teaspoon sea salt flakes
100g dark chocolate chips
  (70% cocoa solids minimum)

Preheat the oven to 160°C fan/180°C/gas 4 and butter and line a 26cm round pie dish or similarly volumed rectangular roasting tin with non-stick baking or greaseproof paper.

Beat the sugar, butter and chopped sage leaves together, then whisk in the eggs. Stir in the flour, baking powder and $^1\!/_2$ teaspoon of sea salt flakes until evenly incorporated, then quickly stir through the chocolate chips.

Alternatively, put everything into a food processor except the chocolate chips and blitz quickly until smooth. Remove the blade, then stir the chips through.

Flatten the cookie dough into the prepared tin, then scatter over the remaining sage leaves and sea salt flakes. Transfer to the oven and bake for 20–25 minutes, until just firm on top – the inside should still be soft. (Check after 15 minutes if you've used a very large roasting tin and the cookie dough has gone in thinly.)

Serve warm, ice cream optional. This reheats very well in slices.

BLACKBERRY & PISTACHIO CAKE

In this dense, rich cake, the pistachio gives an almost baklava-like flavour and works perfectly with the blackberries. David Loftus, the photographer for this book, very kindly said that if he'd been served a little square of this in a Michelin-starred restaurant, he'd have been very happy, so consider impressing your friends with it after dinner. Best eaten the day it is made, on account of the fruit.

Serves: 8
Prep: 10 minutes
Cook: 25 minutes

150g unsalted, shelled pistachios
170g softened unsalted butter,
  plus more for the tin
170g golden caster sugar
3 free-range eggs
30g self-raising flour
1 teaspoon baking powder
200g blackberries,
  halved if very large
Icing sugar, to dust

CHANGE IT UP: For a gluten-free version of the cake, leave out the flour and increase the amount of ground pistachios by 20g, to 170g in total. Make sure your baking powder is gluten-free.

Preheat the oven to 160°C fan/180°C/gas 4, and line and butter a 28 x 22cm roasting or baking tin with non-stick baking or greaseproof paper. Blitz the pistachios in a food processor, spice grinder or Nutribullet until very finely ground (but don't over-blitz, or they'll get oily).

Beat the butter and sugar together until smooth, then whisk in the eggs. Stir in the ground pistachios, flour and baking powder and mix briefly until combined.

Tip the cake batter into the prepared tin and dot with the blackberries. Transfer to the oven and bake for 25 minutes, until the cake is risen, firm to the touch, and a skewer inserted into a non-blackberry bit comes out clean. Do not panic if the cake has risen like a glossy quilted blanket to hide all your blackberries – this will particularly happen with small berries – they're still there and the cake will taste delicious.

Let the cake cool in the tin for 5 minutes before transferring it, with its paper, to a wire rack to cool down. Dust with icing sugar before serving.

POMEGRANATE YOGURT CAKE

I love the texture of a cake made with yogurt instead of butter and this version is quite unusual, with fresh pops of flavour from the pomegranate seeds which contrast with the undertones of dark caramel and acidity from the molasses. A Persephone-in-the-underworld cake.

Serves: 8
Prep: 10 minutes
Cook: 20–25 minutes

80ml olive oil
125g full-fat natural yogurt
60ml pomegranate molasses
2 large free-range eggs
90g soft dark brown sugar
$1/2$ teaspoon ground cinnamon
200g self-raising flour
1 scant teaspoon baking powder
1 pomegranate, seeds only

FOR THE ICING
3 heaped tablespoons icing sugar
$1/2$ tablespoon water

Preheat the oven to 160°C fan/180°C/gas 4. Whisk the olive oil, yogurt, pomegranate molasses and eggs together, then beat in the sugar. Stir in the cinnamon, flour and baking powder, then spoon into to an 28 x 22cm lined roasting or baking tin lined with non-stick baking or greaseproof paper.

Scatter over half the pomegranate seeds, then transfer to the oven and bake for 20–25 minutes, until a skewer inserted comes out clean. Let it cool in the tin for 5 minutes before transferring to a wire rack.

Mix the icing sugar and water together for the icing, then drizzle this all over the cooled cake. Scatter over the remaining pomegranate seeds before serving.

NOTE: As this cake has fresh fruit in and on it, it's best eaten on the day you make it.

SALTED CHOCOLATE PEANUT BROWNIES

If you're looking for a traybake to take to a party, look no further. Chocolate and peanut might be one of my favourite combinations, and this supersized brownie is absolutely delicious, as well as beautiful. If you're serving it warm as an after-dinner dessert, bring a bowl of crème fraîche to the table, as it's very rich.

Serves: 12+
Prep: 10 minutes
Cook: 15–20 minutes

170ml olive oil
250g soft dark brown sugar
100g dark chocolate, chopped
  (70% cocoa solids minimum)
85g plain flour
85g cocoa powder
140ml milk
4 free-range eggs
75g salted peanuts
50g crunchy peanut butter

Preheat the oven to 160°C fan/180°C/gas 4, and oil and line a 30 x 37cm roasting or baking tin with non-stick baking or greaseproof paper. Melt the olive oil, dark brown sugar and chocolate together in a saucepan. Let it cool down for a minute, then whisk in the flour, cocoa, 100ml of the milk and all of the eggs until smooth.

Stir through three-quarters of the salted peanuts, then transfer to the lined tin. Beat the crunchy peanut butter with the remaining 40ml of milk – it should be the consistency of double cream – then drop spoonfuls over the chocolate batter and swirl them in with the wrong end of a teaspoon. Scatter over the remaining peanuts, then bake for 15–20 minutes until just set on top, but still a little soft inside.

Let the brownie cool in the tin, then cut into squares when cool enough to handle. This will keep well in an airtight box for up to a week – if you can resist that long.

ROASTED APRICOTS WITH A ROSEMARY & HAZELNUT CRUMBLE

I love the combination of fresh apricots with hazelnuts. In this crumble, the rosemary adds a wonderful savoury note. Make it when you see the first boxes of apricots arrive in the summer. Any leftovers are an instant roasted fruit-and-granola breakfast the next day.

Serves: 6
Prep: 10 minutes
Cook: 25 minutes

10 large apricots, halved
30g soft light brown sugar,
    plus 2 tablespoons
30g softened unsalted butter
30g oats
30g plain flour
30g hazelnuts, roughly chopped
2 sprigs of fresh rosemary, leaves
    finely chopped
Crème fraîche, Greek yogurt,
    clotted cream, double cream
    or ice cream, to serve

Preheat the oven to 180°C fan/200°C/gas 6. Tip the apricots into a roasting tin or baking dish large enough to hold all the fruit in a single layer, then toss with the 2 tablespoons of soft light brown sugar and set aside while you sort out the crumble topping.

Beat the butter and 30g of sugar together until soft, then stir in the oats, flour, roughly chopped hazelnuts and rosemary. Work together with your fingers until you have a rough crumble texture, then scatter this over the apricots.

Transfer to the oven and roast for 25 minutes, until the crumble topping is golden brown and the apricots are cooked (they should yield when you prod them with a fork).

Serve hot, with any of the suggested accompaniments. Cold clotted cream is particularly nice, or Greek yogurt for breakfast the next day.

TIP: You can easily make this in advance, cool and refrigerate it, then warm it through in the oven for 10–15 minutes or so in an oven preheated to 150°C fan/170°C/gas 3 before serving.

CINNAMON CHERRY CLAFOUTIS

Clafoutis is the perfect dish to finish a dinner party – lighter than a cake, more interesting than a crème caramel – think of it as a smooth, baked, cherry-flecked custard. Traditionally a clafoutis is flavoured with vanilla, but I prefer cinnamon, not least because you can then add a crisp, non-canonical cinnamon-sugar topping. It's very good served with extra-thick double cream or caramel ice cream. (Do make sure to use full-fat milk in the recipe, it makes all the difference.)

Serves: 8
Prep: 10 minutes
Cook: 30 minutes

650g cherries, washed, stalks
    removed (think about
    using frozen out of season)
90g caster sugar
25g unsalted butter, melted,
    plus a bit more for the dish
2 large free-range eggs
75g plain flour
1 teaspoon ground cinnamon
300ml full-fat milk
1 lemon, zest only
20g demerara sugar
1 tablespoon icing sugar

NOTE: Some recipes for clafoutis call for the stones to be removed, but this is both time-consuming and unnecessary, as they add flavour as it cooks. Just warn your guests that there are stones in 'because it's authentic' and they can neatly line them up on the sides of their plates.

Preheat the oven to 180°C fan/200°C/gas 6. You'll need a roasting tin or ceramic baking dish (round, oval, doesn't matter) just large enough to hold all the cherries in a single layer. Check, remove the cherries, butter the dish, then return the cherries to it.

Mix the caster sugar with the melted butter in a large bowl until just incorporated, then beat in the eggs. Add the flour and $1/2$ teaspoon of cinnamon, whisk until smooth, then whisk in the milk and lemon zest. Pour this mixture over the cherries, then transfer to the top shelf of the oven and bake for 30 minutes, until the custard is just set and the edges are lightly brown and risen.

Meanwhile, mix the demerara sugar and the rest of the cinnamon together.

Once cooked, scatter the clafoutis with the cinnamon sugar, then let it cool for a good half an hour before serving warm. Sift over the icing sugar and serve with ice cream, crème fraîche or extra-thick double cream.

PECAN CHOCOLATE CHIP BANANA BREAD

This is one of the nicest versions of banana bread I've ever had and it's perfect for vegans, or if you need an emergency bake and are all out of eggs and butter. Credit goes to my friend Alex, who brainstormed this dessert chapter with me at work and very sensibly suggested that I include a banana bread (and the one opposite was made by her for this book's photo shoot too). Hands down one of my favourite cakes.

Serves: 8-10
Prep: 10 minutes
Cook: 20 minutes

3 ripe-to-overripe bananas, mashed (about 300g when peeled)
75ml olive oil
80g soft dark brown sugar
2 clementines, zest and juice
250g self-raising flour
2 teaspoons baking powder
100g vegan dark chocolate (70% cocoa solids minimum) cut into small chunks
100g pecan nuts, roughly broken

NOTE: If you don't already have a preferred vegan dark chocolate, many good-quality dark chocolate bars with 70% or higher cocoa solids are vegan as they don't contain any milk – just check the label if unsure.

Preheat the oven to 160°C fan/180°C/gas 4, and line a medium roasting tin or baking dish with non-stick baking or greaseproof paper.

Whisk the mashed bananas with the olive oil, sugar and clementine zest and juice until fairly smooth, then stir in the flour and baking powder. When they just start to combine, stir through three-quarters of both the dark chocolate and the pecan nuts.

Smooth the batter into the prepared tin (don't worry, it should look pretty doughy), then scatter with the remaining dark chocolate and nuts. Transfer to the oven and bake for 20 minutes, until well risen and a cake tester or skewer inserted in a non-chocolatey area comes out clean.

Let it cool in the tin for 5 minutes before transferring to a wire rack. This is best eaten warm, but will keep in an airtight tin for a two or three days.

GINGERBREAD PEARS

I love ginger, so this recipe incorporates three kinds: ground, fresh and stem. Despite that, it's a very light gingerbread, which works perfectly with the sunbathing penguin-style baked pears. Serve cold for an afternoon snack, or warm to finish off an autumnal dinner with thick double cream or crème fraîche.

Serves: 8
Prep: 10 minutes
Cook: 25–30 minutes

60g unsalted butter, plus more
   for the tin
125g dark brown sugar,
   plus a few extra pinches
2½cm fresh ginger, grated
1 free-range egg
100ml milk
115g self-raising flour
1 teaspoon ground ginger
3 cardamom pods, seeds ground,
   pods discarded
½ teaspoon baking powder
4 slim pears, halved
1 ball of stem ginger in syrup,
   roughly chopped

Preheat the oven to 160°C fan/180°C/gas 4 and line and butter a 28 x 22cm roasting or baking tin with non-stick or greaseproof paper.

Beat the butter and sugar together until smooth, then whisk in the fresh ginger, egg and milk. Stir in the flour, ground ginger, ground cardamom and baking powder and mix briefly until combined.

Tip the gingerbread batter into the lined tin, then arrange the halved pears across the cake as shown opposite. Scatter a pinch of dark brown sugar and a few bits of chopped stem ginger over each pear, then transfer to the oven and bake for 25–30 minutes, until the cake is risen and firm to the touch.

Let the cake cool down in the tin for 5 minutes before transferring it, with its paper, to a wire rack to cool a little. Serve the gingerbread warm or at room temperature.

NOTE: As it has fresh fruit in it, you'll have to store any leftover gingerbread in the fridge. Warm slices through briefly in the oven or microwave before serving.

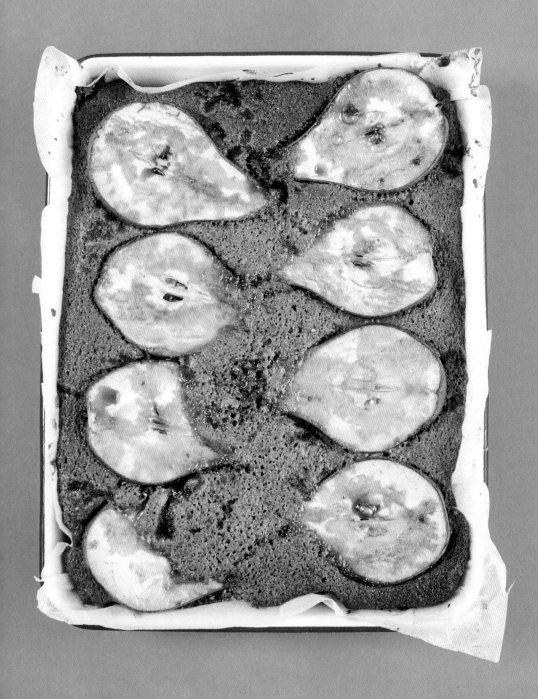

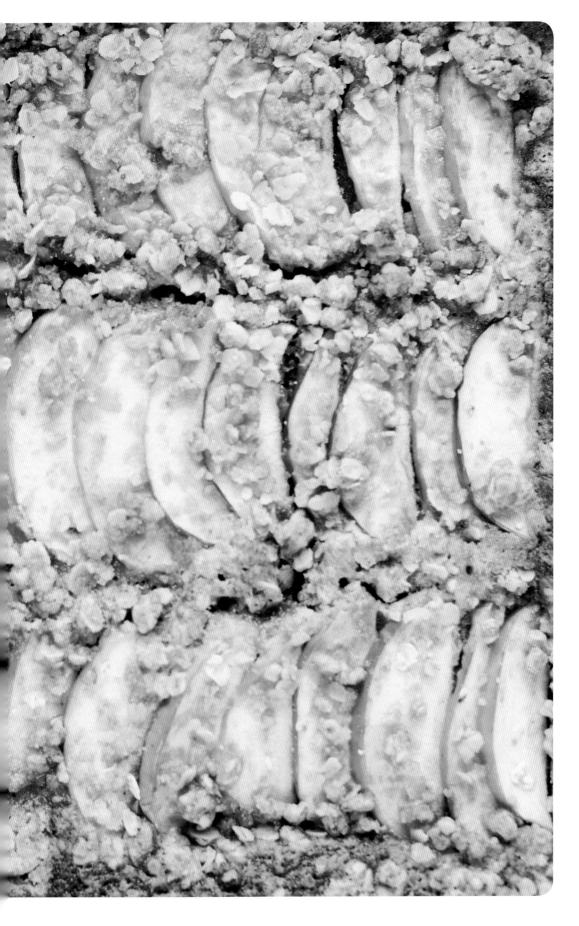

APPLE CRUMBLE CAKE

I feel like a slice of this cake would work at any time of day. Hot out of the oven, it'd also do nicely as pudding on an autumnal evening, with a bowl of crème fraîche on the side.

Serves: 8
Prep: 10 minutes
Cook: 30 minutes

FOR THE CAKE
2 apples, cored and finely sliced
$\frac{1}{2}$ a lemon, juice only
225g softened unsalted butter,
   plus more for the tin
225g soft light brown sugar
4 free-range eggs
225g self-raising flour
$\frac{1}{2}$ teaspoon baking powder
1 teaspoon ground allspice
1 heaped teaspoon ground
   cinnamon

FOR THE CRUMBLE TOPPING
25g demerara sugar (use soft
   light brown sugar if you don't
   already have or won't regularly
   use demerara)
25g softened unsalted butter
25g plain flour
25g oats

Preheat the oven to 180°C fan/200°C/gas 6, and line and butter a 30 x 37cm roasting or baking tin with non-stick or greaseproof paper. Slice the apples and dress them with a little lemon juice to stop them going brown.

Beat the butter and sugar together until smooth, then whisk in the eggs, one by one. Gently stir in the flour, baking powder and spices until just combined.

Transfer the cake batter into the lined tin, and top with the sliced apples in a design of your choice. I like to make them slightly overlapping, as opposite.

Beat the demerara sugar and butter together, then stir in the flour and oats and work with your fingertips into a rough crumble. Scatter this over the cake, then transfer to the oven and bake for 30 minutes, until the topping is golden brown and a skewer inserted into the cake comes out clean.

Let the cake cool in the tin for 5 minutes before lifting it out with its paper on to a wire rack to cool down. Serve warm with crème fraîche, or at room temperature.

CARAMELISED BANANA & THYME TARTE TATIN

I would always suggest that you keep an emergency roll of puff pastry in the fridge and, if you do, this incredibly quick four-ingredient dessert is just the thing to serve if you need a pudding in a hurry. The caramelised bananas work beautifully with the thyme. Serve with a scoop of vegan vanilla or coconut ice cream.

Serves: 6 generously
Prep: 10 minutes
Cook: 25 minutes

1 x 320g ready-rolled vegan
   puff pastry sheet
70g dark brown sugar
3–5* just-ripe to underripe
   bananas, sliced into $\frac{1}{2}$ cm coins
5–6 sprigs of fresh lemon thyme
Vegan vanilla or coconut ice
   cream, to serve

* The number you'll need will depend on the size of the bananas – buy 5, and eat the others if you don't need them for the tart.

Preheat the oven to 180°C fan/200°C/gas 6. Lay the pastry in a roasting tin (you can leave it on the baking paper that it comes wrapped in), ideally one just the right size for the pastry to start coming up the sides of the tin. Prick the base all over with a fork, then scatter over half the brown sugar, leaving a 1cm border around the edges.

Arrange the sliced banana coins on top as close together as you can (they'll shrink on cooking), then scatter thickly with the remaining dark brown sugar and the sprigs of lemon thyme.

Transfer the tart to the oven and bake for 25 minutes, until the pastry is crisp and golden brown. Don't panic if the tart has risen in the middle, just prod it with a fork until it subsides, then gently tip the tin from side to side so the caramel is evenly distributed. Let it cool down for 10 minutes – it'll help set the caramel for a crisp base – then serve with vegan ice cream on the side.

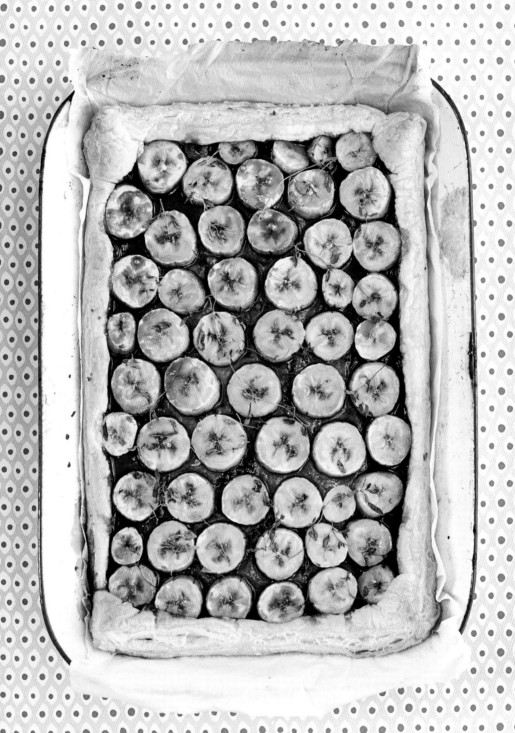

COFFEE & BAILEYS CAKE

Coffee with Baileys was my late godmother Mamie's favourite drink and was invariably offered to me on visits, though once she drew into her nineties, I'd head into the kitchen to make it for us instead. I reckon she'd have approved of this wonderfully light coffee cake, spiked with Baileys and perfect for an afternoon chat.

Serves: 10
Prep: 10 minutes
Cook: 25 minutes

175g unsalted butter, plus more
    for the tin
160g soft light brown sugar
3 free-range eggs
175g self-raising flour
1/2 teaspoon baking powder
2 teaspoons good instant coffee
    (I like Nescafé Azera)
25ml boiling water
50ml Baileys

FOR THE ICING
75g icing sugar
30ml Baileys

NOTE: For Mamie's coffee, take 2 mugs of full-fat milk and heat in the microwave for 3 minutes. Carefully remove, then stir 2 teaspoons of good coffee powder into each mug. Add a splash of Baileys, stir, then serve. It will be too hot to drink for quite a while, so there's lots of time to have a nice chat with your coffee-companion in the meantime.

Preheat the oven to 160°C fan/180°C/gas 4 and line and butter a 28 x 22cm roasting or baking tin, with non-stick baking or greaseproof paper.

Beat the butter and sugar together until smooth, then whisk in the eggs, one by one. Stir in the flour and baking powder, then make up the coffee with the boiling water and stir in the Baileys. Tip this into the cake batter and gently stir until the mixture is smooth.

Transfer the cake batter into the lined tin, then bake for 25 minutes until the cake is risen, firm to the touch and a skewer inserted comes out clean. Let it cool in the tin for 5 minutes before gently lifting it out, with its paper, to cool.

Once the cake is cool, mix the icing sugar and Baileys together to make a thin, pourable icing. Drizzle it over the cake and let the icing set before serving.

A NOTE ON PLATING

The beauty of roasting tin dinners that they're oven-to-table dishes, where everyone piles in and helps themselves. However, if you're doing dishes from the Date Night chapter or the starters from Feed a Crowd, you may wish to 'plate up' before taking your dishes through to the table (though this is of course by no means necessary).

You could write a book on exactly why some plates are aesthetically pleasing and some aren't (and incidentally, my friend and fellow food stylist Frankie Unsworth has done just that – *The New Art of Cooking* – which I'd recommend to anyone interested in making food look as delicious as it tastes).

So, I have scattered examples of how I would plate up a dish attractively though the book and would limit my advice to the following:

ODD NUMBERS

Three or five things on a plate look better than two or four. For example, the roasted fig salad on page 86 or the nectarine and goat's cheese salad on page 130 work beautifully as dinner party starters and will look best if you put an odd amount of fruit on the plate.

ASYMMETRY

Food looks nice off centre on plates, you don't have to arrange everything in the middle. For example, if I was plating the pistachio crusted lamb (page 112) or the pomegranate duck (page 16), I would put a pile of the vegetables or grains slightly off-centre in the middle of the plate and then lay the slices of lamb or duck on the other side.

LEAVES AND HERBS

Keep them in the fridge and dress with your oil and citrus dressing just before plating up, so they don't wilt. If you're putting something like chopped mint leaves through a dish, like the pomegranate duck (see page 116), consider pinching out the little mint tips to scatter over the dish just before serving.

GARNISHES

If there are good-looking elements in a dish that you'd usually stir through (like pomegranate seeds, chopped nuts, chopped herbs), reserve a pinch of each to scatter over your plate just before serving. Also, freshly ground black pepper magically brings a plate together. (Don't be too enthusiastic with this on date night.)

WARM PLATES

Visually, these make no difference. But I dislike hot food on cold plates as much as everyone else hates burning their hands on too-hot plates. The answer? Run your plates under a hot tap to get the chill off before drying and plating up.

INDEX

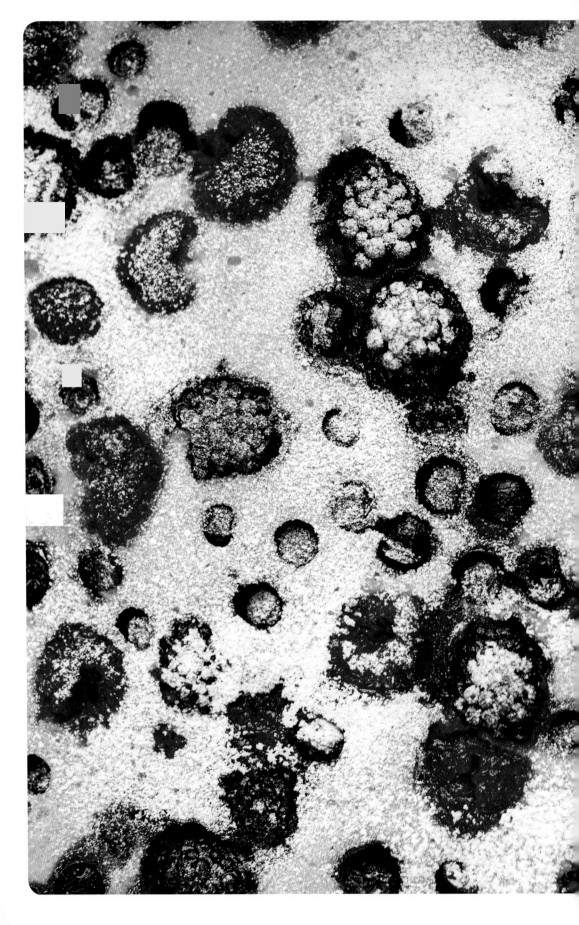

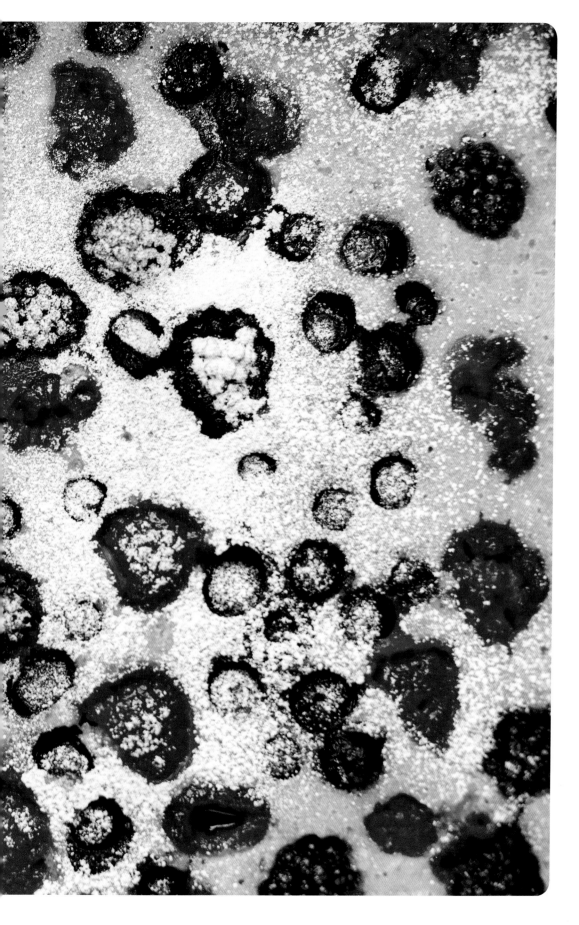

This book wouldn't have happened without Rowan Yapp, the editor with the patience of a saint. Thank you for getting this book off the ground – your enthusiasm is what created mine. Thank you to Harriet Dobson, Sapphire Rees and everyone on the VINTAGE team who has helped on this book and been so amazingly positive about the *Roasting Tin* books.

Pene Parker, this book's designer and art director – thank you so much for being wonderful to work with as always, and for introducing the brilliant prints into the mix. David Loftus, thank you so much for making the food look so beautiful in this book, and to both you and Ange for being lovely to work with. And to Alex Dorgan, for helping me to cook all the dishes in the book for the photo shoot – you are an absolute legend. The kitchen and every other place are much more fun when you are around.

I must shout out to the independent bookshops who have been incredibly supportive about the *Roasting Tin* books. Eric at Books for Cooks, Janet, Helen and Jessica at The Corsham Bookshop and Cate and Nash at Much Ado Books – it has encouraged me no end in writing this book to know that the first two have been so popular and helpful for your customers. I do hope that you, and they, enjoy this book as much as the others.

To my friends and recipe testers, Emma Drage, James Mutton, Danielle Adams Norenberg, Christine Beck, Laura & John Hutchinson, Rosanna Breckner, Ruby Tandoh & Leah Pritchard, Padmini Iyer & Mohit Dalwadi, thank you so much for your willingness to try out the new recipes, your very thorough and helpful feedback, and for being brilliant friends through the year.

My family, Vijay, Parvati and Padmini Iyer, you're the best and most supportive family a person could have – and in the case of Mum and Padz, you're also very helpful recipe testers! Ross, thank you for trying every dish in the book, it meant a lot that when you put your fork down after the very last dish, you said that the recipes in this book were the best I've ever written.

This book is for Mamie, my late godmother. She took us on holidays to the seaside, made the most extraordinarily good fried chicken and potatoes, and looked out for us well into her nineties. Her recipe for coffee with Baileys, and a cake inspired by the same, is the last recipe in this book.

Rukmini is a food stylist and author of the bestelling cookbooks *The Roasting Tin* and *The Green Roasting Tin*. When she's not styling, cooking or entertaining, she can usually be found reading by the riverside and filling her balcony and flat with more plants than they can hold. She is currently researching her next cookbook.

THE ROASTING TIN SERIES

THE ROASTING TIN
SIMPLE ONE DISH DINNERS
RUKMINI IYER

**THE GREEN
ROASTING TIN**
VEGAN & VEGETARIAN ONE DISH DINNERS
RUKMINI IYER

**THE QUICK
ROASTING TIN**
30 MINUTE ONE DISH DINNERS
RUKMINI IYER

NOW AVAILABLE